COUNSELLING IN CRIMINAL JUSTICE

DAVENPORT

· COUNSELLING IN CONTEXT ·

Series editors
Moira Walker and Michael Jacobs
University of Leicester

Counselling takes place in many different contexts: in voluntary and statutory agencies; in individual private practice or in a consortium; at work, in medical settings, in churches and in different areas of education. While there may be much in common in basic counselling methods (despite theoretical differences), each setting gives rise to particular areas of concern, and often requires specialist knowledge, both of the problems likely to be brought, but also of the context in which the client is being seen. Even common counselling issues vary slightly from situation to situation in the way they are applied and understood.

This series examines eleven such areas, and applies a similar scheme to each, first looking at the history of the development of counselling in that particular context; then at the context itself, and how the counsellor fits into it. Central to each volume are chapters on common issues related to the specific setting and questions that may be peculiar to it but could be of interest and value to counsellors working elsewhere. Each book will provide useful information for anyone considering counselling, or the provision of counselling in a particular context. Relationships with others who work in the same setting whether as counsellors, managers or administrators are also examined; and each book concludes with the author's own critique of counselling as it is currently practised in that context.

Current and forthcoming titles

Elsa Bell: *Counselling in Further and Higher Education*
John Brazier: *Counselling at Work*
Judith Brearley: *Counselling and Social Work*
Dilys Davies: *Counselling in Psychological Services*
Patricia East: *Counselling in Medical Settings*
David Lyall: *Counselling in the Pastoral and Spiritual Context*
Judith Mabey and Bernice Sorensen: *Counselling for Young People*
Janet Perry: *Counselling for Women*
Gabrielle Syme: *Counselling in Independent Practice*
Nicholas Tyndall: *Counselling in the Voluntary Sector*
Brian Williams: *Counselling in Criminal Justice*

COUNSELLING IN CRIMINAL JUSTICE

Brian Williams

OPEN UNIVERSITY PRESS
Buckingham · Philadelphia

Open University Press
Celtic Court
22 Ballmoor
Buckingham
MK18 1XW

and
1900 Frost Road, Suite 101
Bristol, PA 19007, USA

First Published 1996

D Copyright © Brian Williams 1996

All rights reserved. Except for the quotation of short passages for the purpose of criticism and review, no part of this publication may be reproduced, stored in a retrieval system, or transmitted, in any form or by any means, electronic, mechanical, photocopying, recording or otherwise, without the prior written permission of the publisher or a licence from the Copyright Licensing Agency Limited. Details of such licences (for reprographic reproduction) may be obtained from the Copyright Licensing Agency Ltd of 90 Tottenham Court Road, London, W1P 9HE.

A catalogue record of this book is available from the British Library

I ISBN 0 335 19240 8 (pbk)

Library of Congress Cataloging-in-Publication Data
Williams, Brian, 1953–
Counselling in criminal justice/Brian Williams.
p. cm. – (Counselling in context)
Includes bibliographical references and index.
ISBN 0–335–19240–8 (pbk.)
1. Social work with criminals. 2. Criminals—Counseling of.
3. Criminals—Rehabilitation. 4. Victims of crimes—Counseling of.
I. Title. II. Series.
HV7428.W55 1996
365′.66—dc20 95–51060 CIP

Typeset by Graphicraft Typesetters Ltd, Hong Kong
Printed in Great Britain by St Edmundsbury Press Ltd,
Bury St Edmunds, Suffolk

Contents

DAVENPORT

STOCKPORT COLLEGE
LIBRARY

XLR 503 03-06-98

4wk 361.06
076213 WAL

Series editors' preface

The ethos of the law seems diametrically opposed to the ethos of counselling. Lawyers specialize in knowledge of the detailed wording of statutes and common law, arguing clause against clause or precedent against precedent. They sometimes appear to the lay person to be far removed from concern for the human predicaments that lie at the heart of legal arguments. It is the interpretation of the law that appears to supersede all else. The other forces of the law, those who sentence, who enforce the law, or who enforce the sentence, appear to have their sight only on judgement, on punishment, on retribution, on keys and locks, or on rewards for good behaviour. Again, this seems a completely different world from that of the counsellor, where the emphasis is on understanding, on not judging, on helping reparation to be made, and on alleviating inappropriate guilt. The forces of the law may tend to see counsellors as soft, counsellors to see the legal profession, the police, and the criminal justice system as lacking in sensitivity and humanity.

No wonder then, as Brian Williams makes clear, that most counsellors do not allow themselves to get near to the issues raised by working in the legal and criminal justice context. If they are not made anxious by the processes of law, and the austerity of wig and gown, by the clanging of prison doors or even the sight of a police car in the driving mirror, they may instead be contemptuous of those who have chosen a quite different way of contributing to society. Yet counsellors must – if they are to be part of the real world – acknowledge and work with the complex issues of society as a whole, including crime and law enforcement.

As the author of this book implies, blinkered attitudes in counsellors do little for their work with clients. There are few people today who are not in one way or another affected by common crimes such as burglary, theft from or of cars, or vandalism. Counsellors are likely to work with clients whose lives have been deeply affected by abusive behaviour, and much of this behaviour constitutes a legal offence, even if – as is often the case – it has not been dealt with within a legal framework. Trauma and justice, loyalties and agonies, run in parallel. Whether as victim, or as family member, whether as accused or convicted, or as custodian of the law, counsellors cannot avoid situations where their clients encounter serious criminal or legal matters.

It is important to recognize that this is not a book about the legal issues related to confidentiality, or about the legal aspects of practice as a counsellor: these are interesting questions, the former vital, but the latter, especially in anxieties such as litigation, largely hypothetical. Rather, this is a book that takes the counsellor deep into the presence and sometimes the source of misery: into the home of the victim of a crime, into the crisis meeting or telephone call with a woman who has been raped, into the contradictory demands made upon the probation officer, into the prisons and the immense difficulties of holding together a view of correction that can in some way meet the outrage of society with a concern and compassion for those whose behaviour owes at least some of its origins to complex causes. This is very obviously not a book simply for those who work in these particular specialized fields – it is one that every counsellor and therapist will value as opening up areas of life that not only our prison and justice systems, but also our attitudes, so often try to shut away.

Moira Walker
Michael Jacobs

Acknowledgements

This book has been a collaborative effort in many ways. I have to thank Nick Tyndall for the original idea, and for a good deal of generous help and encouragement while it was being written. Michael Jacobs has been a patient series editor, has read and re-read draft chapters and given consistently helpful advice, and I have learnt a great deal from working with him.

My colleagues at Keele and other universities have always been happy to discuss the book as it developed, and some have provided help with particular sections. There is no room to thank everyone, but I must mention the assistance of Lena Dominelli and Lennie Jeffers in Sheffield, and of Val Davies, Mike Kosh, Linda Machin, John McLeod, Chris Phillipson, Ruth Tagg and Ray Woolfe in my department at Keele. All my colleagues endured an increased workload to make possible my semester of study leave. Kathy Kendall of Manchester University and Alison Liebling of Cambridge University Institute of Criminology were also generous with their time.

A number of practitioners were interviewed as part of the research for the book. Some were students on counselling courses at Keele, and they all deserve thanks but are too numerous to be named. People who helped with information about specific organizations and issues included Angela of North Staffordshire Rape Crisis Service, Frank Green, Peter Jenkins, Denis Salter and Peter Tarleton. Many of them spent hours ensuring that I avoided making foolish mistakes, although they cannot be blamed if I have nevertheless done so. Thanks also to Victim Support in North Staffordshire and nationally.

The attempt to give the book a comparative dimension was considerably assisted by a grant from the British Academy, which enabled me to spend several weeks in Canada. The hospitality I received there was extraordinary, and I would like to thank everyone who helped me both academically and personally during a very memorable study tour. The list is far from all-inclusive, but particular thanks are due to Denis and Rhonda Bracken, Harvy Frankel and their colleagues at the University of Manitoba Faculty of Social Work; Ann and Wes Charter and the staff of Community and Youth Corrections in Winnipeg; Karlene Faith, Margaret Jackson, Charles Singer and everyone at Simon Fraser University Department of Criminology; Gerry Minard, David Robinson, Moe Royer, Jack Stewart and John Weekes in the federal Correctional Service and everyone I visited in its institutions; Judy Jones of the Law Courts Education Society of British Columbia and the many people she introduced me to; and, of course, all the clients who allowed me to sit in on groups.

All the staff of Keele University Library have been unfailingly willing and inventive, especially those working in the inter-library loan section and on the help desk.

Last but not least, thanks to Sue Roberts, who put up with my moods and distraction during the lengthy process of writing, and assisted in numerous ways, including checking drafts and making numerous helpful suggestions.

· ONE ·

The development of counselling in criminal justice

INTRODUCTION

The criminal justice system is complex and intimidating. Many of its clients are involuntary, and would prefer to have no contact with it. Counsellors who are drawn (sometimes almost as reluctantly as their clients) into working with criminal justice agencies are likely to find the experience confusing and difficult. This book aims to lessen that confusion, by describing the uses to which counselling is currently put in such agencies and by anticipating some of the difficulties likely to be experienced by generic counsellors and their clients in dealing with unfamiliar criminal justice issues and agencies. It also describes the uses of counselling in various parts of the criminal justice system, in the hope of increasing awareness among counsellors of the activities of their colleagues elsewhere in the system.

People who work in criminal justice agencies may find the idea of 'counselling in criminal justice' odd or alien. In the last 20 years criminal justice systems of many countries have largely turned their backs upon trying to rehabilitate offenders. In the process, they have also tended to look to disciplines other than counselling and psychology for insights about how best to work with their clients. Criminal justice has come to be seen as a matter of system management rather than one of personal change, and these are commonly posed as opposites rather than parts of the same whole. In my view this is regrettable, and the book also aims to make a case for retaining a significant place for counselling in criminal justice agencies. Any approach to tackling the problems caused by crime needs to consider the possible potential for changing individual offenders as well as the need to change systems. The discussion is not confined to the treatment of offenders; the role of counselling in staff care and in helping victims of crime is considered alongside offender counselling. If the criminal justice *system* is ever to operate as such, it must surely begin to take a holistic view of the needs of offenders, victims and system personnel. The three groups are rarely discussed alongside each other at present. In this book, the needs of the victims of crime, those of the staff of criminal justice agencies and those of offenders are considered together.

I have chosen to define both 'criminal justice' and 'counselling' fairly broadly. Thus, there is some discussion of agencies with only a peripheral involvement in the criminal justice system (such as the Samaritans and the fire service), and the book looks in some detail at organizations that might not be included in conventional definitions of the criminal justice system (such as Rape Crisis centres). In some cases, this has been dictated by the subject matter; for example, fire service personnel are as likely to suffer post-traumatic stress after major incidents as police officers. At times, the inclusion of agencies like Rape Crisis is deliberately intended to challenge the prevailing rather limited definitions of criminal justice: it is my contention that mainstream agencies deliberately seek to exclude certain organizations and issues from the agenda. Often, they have useful insights to offer, and have pioneered new counselling approaches. They should certainly not be excluded from a discussion of the uses made of counselling in criminal justice merely because they have a radical analysis of the causes of male violence that is uncongenial to senior men in more powerful agencies like the police. I have therefore taken a relaxed view of the boundaries of the criminal justice system, aiming to be inclusive rather than defining it narrowly.

There are also numerous references in the book to the use of 'counselling skills'. By taking such an approach, I seek to demonstrate the relevance of the insights of counselling to criminal justice agencies and their work without being unduly precious about how counselling is defined. Similarly, the book covers group work as well as individual counselling, because the two take place alongside each other in many of the agencies concerned, and group work is sometimes the only (or the dominant) form of intervention taking place. The distinction is always made clear in the text, so that readers are aware of the contexts in which counselling as such is practised, and the differences between these and situations where counselling skills are employed by staff whose main role is not counselling.

COUNSELLING AND THE USE OF COUNSELLING SKILLS

Counselling does not measure its success only in terms of clients' behavioural change. Criminal justice agencies, under pressure from funding bodies, are inclined to use simplistic measures such as rates of recorded reconvictions in an attempt to assess their effectiveness (see Chapter Five, and Jordan 1995). Successful counselling always involves empathy and understanding on the part of the counsellor, and a commitment by clients to work on the issues which are troubling them. It is also characterized by a non-manipulative relationship: at least in the early stages, counsellors avoid giving advice or offering possible definitions of or solutions to clients' problems. If a piece of work meets all three criteria, the counsellor is likely to feel that a successful piece of work has been done.

Counsellors operate under a number of constraints in criminal justice settings, but these three conditions can still be met in certain circumstances. It may be difficult, but people like probation officers and prison chaplains can form empathic, mutually negotiated, non-directive professional relationships with clients. The nature of the obstacles to effective work of this kind forms a major part of the discussion of criminal justice contexts for counselling in the chapters that follow.

Many would argue that an additional criterion should be applied to defining successful counselling, namely, that it is always based upon an explicit contract between the counsellor and the client. The British Association for Counselling has sought to define the practice in this way, but others have pointed out that the world is not always this tidy (Woolfe *et al.* 1989; Brearley 1995). Good practice demands that clients be made aware of the purposeful nature of counselling, and of exactly what is on offer, but this need not always occur in a first interview. In this book, a broader definition is used, recognizing that something recognizable as counselling can take place – at least initially – on an *ad hoc* basis. When the chaplain in Chapter Two (case illustration 2.3) breaks bad news to a prisoner, she is doing more than using counselling skills: she is beginning (or at least offering) a counselling relationship. If the client chooses to continue seeing her, there will be plenty of time later to define the terms of the counselling, as long as the opportunity for this has been properly prepared at the outset.

What is more widespread than the use of counselling in this sense is the use of counselling skills and techniques in criminal justice settings. While the use of such skills by people like probation and police officers is important, it is necessary to distinguish between this and counselling as such. This distinction is made throughout the book, and when references are made to 'counselling skills' this is done deliberately to signal that counselling in the pure sense of meeting all or most of the three criteria just outlined is not under discussion. Police officers taking a statement from the victim of an offence may employ counselling skills, but they could not be said to be counselling the victim. In this context, a police officer might be an appropriate person to act as a counsellor, but collecting information for a prosecution is not part of the counselling process. The power differential between police officer and witness makes this inappropriate, even if it were possible.

These issues of definition are important, and they are discussed further in Chapter Four. They are also considered at greater length in a thoughtful and useful way by Woolfe *et al.* (1989). They point out that counselling is often confused with giving advice and with attempts to impose orthodox views (as in 'debt counselling' or 'substance misuse counselling'), whereas its great strength lies in its rejection of such manipulation. They go on to argue that another strength of counselling is the increasing willingness in recent years to recognize the social and structural aspects of individual problems. This is an issue to which I return in Chapter Six.

CRIMINAL JUSTICE AGENCIES AS SETTINGS FOR COUNSELLING

Although it is normal and commonplace to refer to 'the criminal justice system', it is not always clear what is meant by this. The term is vague and rather elastic; sometimes it refers only to certain agencies, and often those using it do not examine their own assumptions about what it includes and excludes. Does it refer only to formal, statutory organizations, or does it include voluntary organizations and informal associations? In this book, it is used very loosely. Some of the organizations whose work is described would not characterize themselves as part of the criminal justice system: Rape Crisis centres, for example, are independent of the other agencies and they are not answerable to the courts or the police. Nevertheless, they are in constant liaison with other criminal justice agencies and their clientele, and their *raison d'être* arises from the criminal activities of perpetrators (who may or may not be caught and processed by the system). While they do not see themselves as criminal justice agencies, they interact with the system to such an extent that they are in some sense part of it. They are included here because they work with criminal justice clients, they undertake counselling and they have an impact upon other agencies' attitudes to it.

Similarly, Victim Support schemes are seen by their organizers as independent of the more formal agencies; yet they receive almost all their referrals from the police and the courts, and much of their funding from the Home Office. They have a close relationship with the probation service, but they are part of a voluntary body. They are accountable (through their government funding) to the statutory agencies, but not directly answerable to them at a local level. Again, they figure in this book both for pragmatic reasons – they counsel people in contact with the formal criminal justice system – and because they influence the view of counselling taken by other agencies. To the extent that they are seen as offering effective help to the victims of crime, they serve to 'sell' counselling as a useful form of intervention.

Agencies whose primary concern is the welfare of victims of crime have struggled to make their voice heard by the statutory agencies, with some success. Other groups that work with victims, such as Women's Aid and various self-help organizations, do not normally undertake counselling, but their work is touched upon in the book from time to time because of their intimate involvement with criminal justice agencies and their focus upon the needs of victims of crime. They sometimes offer a critique of counselling from the standpoint of insiders, including counsellors' clients, and this is discussed in Chapter Four.

There are several 'mainstream' agencies that everyone agrees are part of the criminal justice system. These include the prison service, the courts, the probation service and the police. Other statutory organizations have a more peripheral role, although they are seen as part of the system for certain purposes. Examples include social services, 'civilian' prison staff such as those working in chaplaincy and psychology services, and psychiatric services. To the extent that they use counselling and counselling skills, these agencies are included in the book.

There is controversy about the extent to which this cluster of distinctive organizations should be seen as a 'system' at all. Failures of communication between the different agencies have been blamed for many of the problems experienced by victims of crime (to give only one example). Variations in the occupational cultures of staff between agencies hinder effective liaison, and misunderstandings inevitably occur. To a certain extent, counselling may offer a common language facilitating effective contact between people in different agencies. While this could easily be overstated, it is a theme which runs through some of the chapters which follow. It can also be argued that the limitations of counselling as an approach to systemic and structural problems must be acknowledged: an individualized response to major social problems such as racism and sexism will not attack the real problems, and may serve to conceal them. This is discussed in Chapter Six.

THE HISTORY OF COUNSELLING IN CRIMINAL JUSTICE SETTINGS

The case is made above for discussing offenders, their victims and those who work with them together in this book. All have the potential to become the clients of counsellors, and I have argued for a holistic approach when discussing their needs. In this section, however, they will be treated separately, as the history of counselling in relation to each group is different, and the differences are revealing in various ways. It would be very difficult to give a coherent account of the development of counselling in so many different and disparate areas without splitting it up in some way.

Other volumes in this series have given accounts of the gradual and logical development of counselling in particular areas (see for example Tyndall (1993) in relation to the voluntary sector, and Brearley (1995) on social work). They have referred to influential writers and practitioners who have had important roles in promoting counselling in those settings. A different approach is taken in the present volume, for a number of reasons. First, the development of counselling in criminal justice systems has been confused and complex: no linear process towards consensus on its usefulness seems to have occurred. So many agencies and countries are potentially involved that a detailed history would be lengthy and confusing. The role of individuals has not been as important in criminal justice settings as the part played by movements – for example, by the women's movement and what has sometimes been called the victims' movement. What follows is, for these reasons, a series of brief, impressionistic histories of the development of counselling in three main areas: work with offenders, work with victims, and staff care. Where appropriate, the accounts of Tyndall (1993) and Brearley (1995) are commended to the reader rather than being repeated here.

Counselling offenders

Attitudes towards crime have changed significantly over the last 200 years, and this has greatly influenced the ways in which offenders are treated. The urban poor were seen as the 'dangerous classes' until relatively recently, and male crime and female prostitution were understood largely in terms of the strange habits and customs of these unfamiliar, pathologized people (Emsley 1994). Judicial punishment was a bloodthirsty attempt to contain the excesses of a threatening underclass. Conditions in prisons were squalid and harsh, and most policy makers saw this as entirely appropriate.

It would be wrong to see penal reform as a gradual process of amelioration leading towards a humane system – not least because our modern prisons mostly remain cruel and sordid, and because there was a genuine religious and moral commitment in the eighteenth and nineteenth centuries to using imprisonment as a way of giving people time to reflect upon their misdeeds and plan for a better future. All the same, there was a slow change in attitudes towards offenders. Imprisonment came increasingly to be seen as a last resort when other, more humane measures had failed, with rehabilitation into an honest life the ideal response to crime. The practicability of attaining this ideal has been challenged since the 1970s, as the effectiveness of rehabilitative approaches has been questioned, but a new optimism is emerging (see below).

Early penal reformers argued, for humanitarian reasons and in the interests of social control, that prisoners and other offenders should receive help and advice, often from church sources, if they showed that they deserved it. The political and moral certainties of these philanthropists were increasingly challenged during the twentieth century, and secular, professional services were gradually created alongside the religious ones, ultimately supplanting them. The probation service, for example, had its roots in the Church of England Temperance Society, but broke its links with the church as state funding became available. By the 1960s it was completely independent, and its services were provided irrespective of clients' perceived deservedness (Williams 1994; Brearley 1995).

After the Second World War, the Criminal Justice Act 1948 reflected earlier progressive thinking in England and Wales, and abolished the more blatantly punitive aspects of the prison system. It also reflected the increasing trend towards rehabilitating individual offenders (Emsley 1994). Psychodynamic concepts initially dominated research and practice, giving way gradually in the criminal justice field to Rogerian approaches which emphasized the need to show empathy with offenders. Later, cognitive and behavioural theories became influential (reflecting the increase in professional attention given to sexual offending). For the first 30 years after the war, there was a substantial political consensus about the need to concentrate upon changing individual offenders, encouraging them to adopt pro-social attitudes rather than simply punishing them. In North America, there was less agreement about this issue, and the debate about crime there has been highly politicized (and emotive) for much longer than in Britain, where it was politicized from the late 1980s. Nevertheless, for a time in the 1960s and 1970s, decarceration strategies commanded widespread support in America and Canada too.

'Social casework' was the Victorian term for social work with individuals. From the 1950s, the term came to be used in a more specialist sense: the relationship between worker and client, and its therapeutic potential, were emphasized. Not only probation officers, but Borstal housemasters and later prison officers at Grendon Underwood and other prisons operating therapeutic regimes saw themselves as caseworkers. Later, prison officers in many prisons became involved in Social Work in Prison schemes, whereby they filtered prisoners' applications for professional help and dealt with many of the requests themselves (see Chapter Two).

Gradually 'casework' with offenders became 'counselling', the terminology changing to reflect new attitudes, just as it had previously done in respect of marital work undertaken by probation workers and marriage guidance counsellors (see Proctor 1991; Tyndall 1993). Work in prisons and in the probation service from the late 1950s was strongly influenced by these developments, and by courses at the Tavistock Institute, the London School of Economics, Leeds University and the Prison Service Staff College, which reflected and promoted the development of what is now called counselling (Tyndall 1994).

There was a substantial setback for those who believed in the individual rehabilitation of offenders when American academics began in the late 1970s to publish research that seemed to show that 'nothing works' (see Chapter Five). This was based upon a serious misinterpretation of the data, but it rapidly gained the status of folk wisdom and did morale in the caring professions a good deal of damage. A decade later, Canadian research questioned the validity of the prevailing pessimism about offender rehabilitation, and was followed by rigorous research in America, Australasia and Europe which pointed to the success of offender counselling under certain conditions. In particular, the use of cognitive and behavioural techniques was consistently linked with effectiveness (see Chapter Five). A new, and perhaps not wholly justified, wave of optimism swept through academia and the professions dealing with offenders. It was, however, informed for the first time by practice-based research that offered pragmatic criteria for focused work with particular types of client as well as proper monitoring of effectiveness.

In response to a lengthy economic crisis, governments in the developed world began in the 1980s to take a more interventional approach to training policy, taking the view that the workforce needed to be trained for generic 'competence' rather than for specific professional tasks, in the name of international competitiveness. This had a profound impact upon training for the police, prison and probation services. One unintended consequence was that 'people skills' began to be downplayed in favour of competence. This trend is discussed in greater depth in Chapters Two and Six (and also by Hayman 1993; Brearley 1995). Just as the climate had become more favourable to offender counselling, other factors skewed the training of professional staff away from an emphasis upon personal skills and one-to-one counselling, but the professions employing counselling were far from happy with this development, as described in the next chapter.

The 1980s also saw something of a backlash in many developed countries against the idea of helping offenders to reform. The criminological ideas of the 'new right' became influential, and legislation based upon the notion of 'just deserts' (or 'an eye for an eye') was passed in England and Wales, the United States and Canada. Elsewhere, more person-centred views prevailed: offender counselling and restorative approaches became a more central part of the criminal justice systems of countries such as New Zealand and France (see Hudson 1993; Morris *et al.* 1993; Consedine 1995; and Chapter Four). At the time of writing, it is difficult to know whether client-centred approaches will prevail – but this book is written in the belief that they have more to offer than simplistic attempts to control the behaviour of offenders by the use of punishment. Sooner or later the true cost of inhumane policies will become apparent (Day 1995; Jordan 1995). There is no doubt that counselling can be effective, and the arguments about this issue are reviewed in Chapter Five.

Restorative approaches to offending, which provide offenders with opportunities to try to restore their victims to their condition before the offence, are emerging in a variety of guises around the world. This trend will be discussed in the next section, as it relates mainly to victims' welfare.

Offenders are now involved in individual counselling in a wide variety of criminal justice settings. The probation order typically involves individual supervision, often in combination with group work or additional, specialist counselling. Prisoners may be involved in one-to-one counselling with a psychologist, a chaplain, a prison probation officer or sometimes a prison officer. These are the most obvious settings for offender counselling, but there are many others, some of which are described in case illustrations later in this book. Whatever the political climate, offender counselling is flourishing.

This has happened largely because of the historical links between probation and social work, and the influence exerted upon the prison service by its in-house psychologists, probation officers and chaplains. Their social work training has ensured that probation officers develop counselling skills (at least until recently: see Chapter Two). The in-service training available to psychologists and chaplains has also emphasized counselling. Although prison officers have had relatively few opportunities for professional development of this kind, those working in counselling roles have largely been trained on the job by probation officers and psychologists.

Offenders have made considerable demands upon the available counselling services, both in prison and in the community: there is no doubt of the demand for non-judgemental, structured counselling help (Williams 1991; Bailey 1995). The arrival of the AIDS epidemic created further demands upon criminal justice professionals, highlighting new training needs (Padel 1995). Prison- and community-based counselling agencies responded by meeting part of the demand themselves and negotiating with specialist voluntary agencies in an attempt to ensure that appropriate services were provided. The involvement of community agencies that also campaigned on sexual health issues and discrimination against people with AIDS was not initially welcomed by all prison staff, but the expertise and direct counselling help they have been able to provide has done a good deal to break down such barriers.

Counselling victims of crime

The women's movement has made an enormous contribution to our understanding of criminal victimization. The most obvious examples are those of rape, child sexual abuse and 'domestic' violence. Feminist campaigning, research and service provision have also influenced policy and practice in relation to the treatment of crime victims more generally. The feminist contribution to our understanding of the process of repeat victimization (whereby the investigation and processing of crime further traumatizes victims), and of the long-term nature of much criminal and family victimization, has much wider implications. Some services, such as Rape Crisis centres, draw directly upon feminist counselling methods, while others reflect the influence of feminism less obviously. Victim Support schemes, for example, have changed the ways in which they work with women after rape, drawing on the lessons of feminist counselling, and frequently use Rape Crisis counsellors to train their own volunteers. The criminal justice system has also begun to make changes in routine practices in response to feminist research and campaigning, as in the new procedures for videotaped evidence in child sexual abuse cases.

Awareness of the needs of the victims of crime is relatively recent. The other main organizations campaigning to change the criminal justice system's approach to victims have been self-help groups and the broader victims' movement. Criminological interest in the victims of crime began in the late 1940s in America, and victimology is now a flourishing discipline in its own right. A victims' movement emerged in America in the early 1970s and in the rest of the developed world over the following decade. Its initial focus was upon the practical needs of crime victims, including the need for financial compensation and to be kept in touch with the progress of the legal case against the offender. Increasingly, victims' organizations have framed the issue in terms of rights as well as needs: NOVA in the United States and (to a lesser extent) the National Association of Victim Support Schemes in Britain have campaigned for better treatment of victims. From an early stage, it became clear that there was a significant minority of crime victims who needed more than practical help and neighbourly concern. Some people react particularly adversely to criminal victimization, and they require counselling as well as support. Victim support agencies have not yet developed sufficiently precise or sophisticated methods of determining which clients are most likely to need long-term support (Maguire 1991), but it may be preferable for some victims to suffer irritation at being referred inappropriately than for others to miss the opportunity altogether. The different wings of the victims' movement have taken a wide variety of approaches to providing counselling.

Indeed, if the phrase 'victims' movement' suggests a united, homogeneous body, this is misleading (Zedner 1994). The range of responses to the perceived need of certain victims for counselling illustrates the diversity of the movement itself. Feminist organizations such as Rape Crisis have developed their own theoretical and practical approaches to counselling, using only female counsellors (see Chapter Two). Some self-help groups (which vary enormously) have encouraged members to train as counsellors so that help can be offered to new members as they join; some distrust the usefulness of counselling and do not encourage members to engage in it; others refer members to Victim Support. An example of the former approach is Support After Murder and Manslaughter, whose committee is active in trying to encourage larger groups like Victim Support to improve their volunteers' awareness of the special needs of the families of murder victims. Victim Support itself has responded to new needs as they have been drawn to its attention (and has initiated much of the research that has revealed such needs). Specialist training is now provided for its volunteers and staff to enable them to offer appropriate counselling to victims of a range of types of offence, and Victim Support has constantly extended itself in response to new needs (Tyndall 1993).

Feminist counselling with crime victims began in response to rape and other forms of male violence. First in America, and then elsewhere, the provision of battered wives' hostels and Rape Crisis centres as places of refuge was followed by arrangements for counselling. Abused women needed safe places to shelter, but they also had more deep-seated problems arising from their victimization; many were depressed or suicidal, and most needed a sympathetic and supportive hearing while they repeatedly recounted the details of what they had suffered. The most severely traumatized suffered intrusive memories of their abuse and intense anger, which they often found very frightening (Walker 1990). In response, the women's movement drew upon the existing knowledge of counselling techniques and supplemented it with a repertoire of specifically feminist methods and theories (see Chapters Three and Four, and for details of feminist counselling methods, see Chaplin (1988), Perry (1993), Barnes and Henessy (1995), Taylor (1995)).

In England, police mistreatment of women reporting rape was highlighted by the intense public reaction to a powerful television documentary made by Roger Graef in 1982. The film showed the insensitivity and disbelief that characterized police interviewing of complainants at that time. In the short term, it probably discouraged women from reporting rapes, but substantial changes were made fairly quickly across the country in police methods of investigating not only rape but other sexual offences (Zedner 1994). Feminist pressure, and the involvement of feminist counselling agencies in police training, helped to achieve this by challenging the prevailing myths about rape. Knowledge about rapists and men who abuse their partners and children was also augmented by those working with victims and offenders, and feminists began to become involved in applying their understanding of the motivation of violent men in offender counselling (Dobash *et al.* 1995). Information collected by feminist agencies was thus fed back into efforts to alter offenders' attitudes and behaviour towards women.

Feminist understanding also contributed to greater sophistication in the treatment of people abused as children. This enabled counsellors to move on from the victim-blaming that was common in psychotherapeutic treatment, and to help survivors of childhood abuse move forward from self-blame and guilt (Barnes and Henessy 1995). Feminist counsellors were able to empathize with the feelings of powerlessness, rage and manipulation experienced by abused children in a way other caring professionals had rarely achieved. These developments did a great deal to promote the wider acceptance of victim counselling in its early days (Perry 1993).

Alternative approaches to family violence and other types of criminal victimization have been developed in New Zealand and Australia. New Zealand's system of family group conferences tries to combine attention to the needs of victims and those of young offenders, and draws upon traditional Maori justice (Morris *et al.* 1993; Consedine 1995). When this process succeeds, it appears to have a cathartic effect for both offenders and victims, leading to truly restorative and negotiated penalties. The indications are that many victims are willing to give young offenders another chance, but that some feel inhibited about expressing their true feelings in a large meeting where the consensus often favours restorative rather than retributive approaches (Morris *et al.* 1993). Giving victims rights is one thing, but providing them with such a crucial place in decision making about the ways in which offences are resolved may place them under considerable and unwelcome pressure, although the system might be made to work for them if proper resources are provided for counselling (Lee and Searle 1993). Most victims of serious crime need to work through their feelings of anger and loss before they want to consider the needs of 'their' offender. Given that opportunity, many have displayed remarkably forgiving attitudes.

A similar system has now been introduced in Australia with adult offenders, where it is claimed that the community conference approach evens out inequalities between offenders and victims as adults and young people, men and women, and members of different races, although it is acknowledged that the problems experienced in

New Zealand may well be replicated by the Australian system (Braithwaite and Daly 1994). There is clearly a need to adapt such innovations to fit the dominant culture when importing them to a new country, and time will tell whether the Australian experiment is successful. Similar initiatives are under way in Canada (see Bracken 1995; and Chapter Four).

For a variety of reasons, black people in Britain and other countries where they are in a minority are likely to suffer criminal victimization to a disproportionate extent (see Smith 1995). Arrangements for counselling victims of crime must be made in ways sensitive to the needs of people who are racially harassed and assaulted, or targeted for victimization for racial reasons, and Victim Support schemes are increasingly providing specialized training to enable staff and volunteers to respond appropriately. Awareness of the racial dimensions of counselling has developed comparatively recently (d'Ardenne and Mahtani 1989), and it is an aspect frequently omitted in discussions of victims of crime (Senior 1993a). Maguire (1991) suggests that this neglect of race issues has arisen in England and Wales from the dominance of police definitions of the nature of crime and victimization, but more should be done to prioritize racial harassment and the preparation of counsellors to help its victims. Counsellors cannot simply blame others for the lack of ethnically sensitive provision.

Black people do not only suffer more criminal victimization because of where they live and their economic circumstances; they are also deliberately targeted because they are black. The experience of Victim Support's pilot projects for helping racial harassment victims in London was interesting for a number of reasons. First, its staff found that there were already some self-help arrangements in place, and they wisely took care to avoid stepping on the toes of the organizations that had set these up. Secondly, the counsellors found that they could not simply deal with victims one to one; they also had to become involved in liaison, outreach and development work. This was partly because the police did not refer some victims to the project, but also because the individual casework revealed issues concerning the local housing departments, schools and general practitioners' surgeries that had to be dealt with to prevent further victimization. There was also a need for liaison with the existing black community organizations, particularly in order to deal with widespread initial suspicion of Victim Support itself, but also to engage with their interpreters and community workers (Kimber and Cooper 1991).

This illustrates the need for a degree of activism by counsellors working in controversial areas of practice. Counselling does not exist outside of society, and counselling agencies sometimes have to engage with their social context in ways similar to those described in the report of the racial harassment pilot projects. The authors note that in many cases 'more time was spent on liaison than on actual contact with the victim' – and that this emphasis was often at victims' initiative (Kimber and Cooper 1991: 38).

Counselling practitioners

Although shell shock has been a recognized mental health problem for decades, the idea that workers other than soldiers suffer reactions to their environment sufficiently extreme to merit counselling support is a comparatively recent one. The tendency of nurses who were under pressure to avoid direct personal contact with patients by erecting social defences and hiding behind rituals was observed by Menzies (1960), as part of a much wider study of defences against anxiety, but she was inclined to see these as an example of social pathology. She did not dwell upon the individual psychological needs being expressed by the nurses' behaviour.

It was only after a series of large-scale disasters that the value of occupational subcultures in protecting care workers against stress began to be recognized. Another consequence was that the personal needs of staff in the aftermath of disasters became clearer, and treatment methods were developed to deal with post-traumatic stress and with less pronounced but nonetheless painful reactions. The everyday pressures which can lead to staff burn-out were taken increasingly seriously as the real cost of replacing trained staff became apparent. Parallel with this development, there was an increasing interest in some parts of the criminal justice system in improving blue-collar workers' job satisfaction in order to avoid alienation and burn-out (see the discussion of the Better Jobs Initiative in the prison service in England and Wales in Chapter Two).

After an air crash in the Antarctic in 1979, the reactions and the psychological needs of rescue workers were systematically studied, perhaps for the first time (Kinchin 1993). Subsequent events at Bhopal in India, Three Mile Island in the United States, the Hillsborough, Ibrox Park and Bradford football stadium disasters in the United Kingdom, the King's Cross fire in London and a series of ferry sinkings in various parts of Europe provided all too much data for further large-scale studies of post-traumatic stress.

Taking the Lockerbie aeroplane bomb disaster as an example, it is clear that the organizations involved in recovering the bodies and dealing with the bereaved learnt valuable lessons from the process, which have been widely shared within the professions and services involved. What also became clear was that many people with less direct involvement in the disaster also experienced post-traumatic stress, and that their needs largely went unmet. People like medical records clerks and the public utilities workers who had to go and turn off the gas and electricity in the demolished houses were extremely distressed, but were not seen as needing counselling. Their stress manifested itself in indirect ways such as through excessive smoking and drinking, marital problems, viral illnesses and heart attacks. The connection with the disaster was made only subsequently. Such events require a massive mobilization of psychological support as well as (or partly replacing) the huge military-style response by the uniformed services at the scene (Salter 1995).

This lesson has partly been learnt, in that large employers (including the emergency services) increasingly provide staff counselling schemes. This is discussed in greater detail in Chapter Two. They also tend increasingly to see the need for continuous monitoring of stress levels and of staff morale and psychological health, if only because of the high cost of replacing staff who leave. The role of counselling agencies is described in case illustrations in Chapter Four. In Chapter Two, the place of counselling in criminal justice agencies is reviewed in more general terms, and in Chapter Three the limitations of and the opportunities afforded by working in such settings are considered.

A NOTE ON TERMINOLOGY

In this chapter, the vagueness (or the useful elasticity) of some terms has been noted. The 'criminal justice system' can include or exclude particular agencies depending upon who is using the phrase, without such implications necessarily being made explicit. In what follows, efforts are made to avoid ambiguity of this kind, by highlighting any such exclusivity and by using the term inclusively. 'Counselling' has also been distinguished from the less specific 'counselling skills' in the interests of clarity.

In keeping with recent practice, I have used the word 'black' throughout the book to refer to anyone who experiences discrimination or exclusion by white people on racial grounds. Where this terminology might have led to differences within black communities being overlooked, alternative descriptions such as 'Asian' have been used, but in general terms it has been assumed that black people share certain experiences at the hands of whites, and that ethnically sensitive service provision needs to take account of this.

Unlike some other writers, I have used 'race' without inverted commas, although I am well aware of the problematic nature of the term. The concept has its roots in imperialist thinking about the superiority of white people, and in biological science it is a discredited notion, but it nevertheless has explanatory power when we discuss relations between black and white people (Mason 1995).

I am also aware that 'racism' is a contentious idea. I have written elsewhere about the evidence that the criminal justice system is a site of institutional racism (Dominelli *et al.* 1995), and the arguments for and against this view are not rehearsed again here. It seems to me that the systematic failure to provide services which are accessible to and suitable for black people is a continuing problem of the criminal justice systems of Europe, Australasia and North America. Combined with those systems' common failure to address the over-representation of black people in their prisons and mental health facilities, this makes it difficult to challenge the assertion that criminal justice agencies are part of the problem of institutional racism. Where there are grounds for thinking they may also be or become part of the solution, this has been highlighted in the chapters that follow. Ethical counselling has to be based upon a determination to oppose racism, and this is discussed briefly in Chapter Six.

· TWO ·

The context of counselling in criminal justice

Those engaged in counselling prisoners, probation clients and victims of crime are unlikely to be called counsellors, and may not regard counselling as a central part of their role, as we have seen. Nevertheless, they are working in sensitive situations, often with damaged people, and they need to be able to call upon a repertoire of sophisticated skills. Some of them have access to appropriate training, but others have to seek it out in their own time and at their own expense. The status of counselling and counselling skills varies tremendously from one criminal justice agency to another, as does the amount of training made available to staff and volunteers, and this has implications for the extent to which they are allowed to work autonomously and in accordance with their own values. The criminal justice agencies are complex bureaucracies, and it is important to be clear about one's professional and personal values when working with or within them.

LOCATIONS OF COUNSELLING IN LEGAL CONTEXTS

Probation work

Where, then, does counselling in legal contexts take place, and who undertakes it? As Judith Brearley has observed (1995), there are overlaps and potential conflicts between counselling and social work. Social workers regarded casework as the mainstay of their work in the 1960s, and this mainly drew upon what would now be described as counselling skills and theory. There are similar overlaps and contradictions between social work and probation work, and this has become a political and ideological battleground during the 1990s. Probation officers also described their practice as casework for many years, and they have hitherto been trained as and alongside social workers, identifying professionally with the values of social work, but in England and Wales the government set its face against this in 1995, intending to try to distance probation training and practice from social work.

Meanwhile, social work itself has changed enormously in response to the community care legislation, privatization and managerialism. Social workers and probation officers find themselves acting increasingly as 'case managers' rather than working directly with clients (Simiç 1995). Counselling has been marginalized in their training, and when long-term work is called for, it is more likely to be provided by volunteers or workers in partner agencies than by probation officers.

Case illustration 2.1

Mark, who is 25, is appearing in court in four weeks' time charged with serious sexual offences against a boy of 13. When interviewed by John, the probation officer writing the report for the court, he denies that anything violent or improper took place: the boy is a family friend and Mark says he loves him, and that sexual activity occurred naturally. He has been advised by his solicitor to admit the offences, but he does not accept that he should be punished or sentenced to any kind of treatment: he feels that the offence is a technical one, the result of an outdated law. Nevertheless, he does accept that he has broken the law.

John talks to him about the various sentencing options available to the court, and they eventually agree that the pre-sentence report should propose a probation order with a condition of attending a group for male sex offenders. As well as engaging in this group work, Mark would be required to see John regularly for individual counselling for the whole period of the order. Mark is extremely reluctant to engage in such a group, but John makes it clear that he is likely to face a prison sentence if he does not consent. Mark says he will comply with the conditions of any order the court decides to make: he would rather die than go to prison. John arranges for him to be seen by colleagues at the probation centre, who carry out a brief assessment and submit an addendum to John's court report saying that Mark is suitable for a probation order with a condition of attendance at the centre.

When Mark's case comes to court, he is sentenced to two years in prison. John telephones the prison probation officer and medical officer warning them that Mark may be suicidal, and he is interviewed by a prison doctor the next day but placed on 'normal location' rather than in the prison hospital. Two weeks later he is transferred to the vulnerable prisoners' unit of another prison where there is a Sex Offender Treatment Programme. Mark is invited by the prison probation officer to take part in a group intended to address his offending behaviour. He is reluctant, but has been told by other prisoners that his chances of early release would be prejudiced by refusing. He has also begun to worry about his long-term future if he continues to appear in court, so he eventually agrees to take part in the programme.

Claudia, the prison-based probation officer, talks to Mark and decides to put his name forward for a group which is due to start soon afterwards. She has her doubts about the degree of his commitment to address his offending behaviour, but she has seen some young men in similar circumstances respond well, and she sees some potential for change. She talks to the prison psychologist who runs the group with two prison officers, and suggests that Mark, as a first-time prisoner, may benefit from the programme but may need quite a lot of attention owing to his vulnerability to bullying.

Meanwhile, the victim of the offences is assessed by his social worker and referred to a group for sexually abused adolescents (which is run by a specialist unit at the local hospital).

This case illustrates some of the constraints upon probation officers when they see a need for counselling. Their clientele is selected by the courts, and their contact with any individual may be only very short term. While considerable skill is needed in making an appropriate assessment in the time available in just a couple of interviews – whether for a court report or a group-work programme – officers do not always have direct experience of all the facilities to which they might make referrals. As it happened, in the case above, John had worked in a probation centre in the past, and Claudia had co-led a previous group for sex offenders in the prison, but neither had an opportunity to engage in direct work with Mark over any sustained period.

Sometimes there is considerable dissatisfaction among the professionals with the counselling being offered to clients. The Sex Offender Treatment Programme is a case in point: it was widely criticized by probation officers when first introduced. The introductory training provided for the staff delivering the programme was described as brief and superficial, and the exercises used during the groups were thought to be rigid, unimaginative and unlikely to address deep-seated sexist attitudes held by staff and offenders. From the beginning, there were conflicts between prison psychologists, uniformed staff and probation officers about the underlying values of the programme and about the relative scarcity of resources allocated to it (Cowburn 1993; Brown 1994; Sampson 1994). Unfortunately, this programme was introduced simultaneously in a number of prisons and became the only one available to most inmates, replacing quite sophisticated provision in some establishments.

These criticisms were subsequently heeded, and there is anecdotal evidence that some improvements have been made to the programme. All the same, a substantial new programme was introduced in a standardized form without sufficient consultation or preparation, and it is not surprising that staff responded unfavourably. It appears that the prison service bureaucracy, in its anxiety to show that it was dealing with a perceived problem, neglected to use its own staff's existing expertise sufficiently. When change is imposed in this way, it is bound to cause unproductive anxiety and inter-professional boundary disputes, and these are not in the interests of those in need of help (Woodhouse and Pengelly 1991).

Case illustration 2.2

Danny is 18. He is a heavily convicted burglar and 'TWOCer' (car thief). He has just been in court for further, similar offences and, although he has served a term in custody in the past, he has been ordered to attend an intensive group at his local probation centre. The group, run by two probation officers who have received special training, is based on the 'reasoning and rehabilitation' programmes developed in Canada (Ross and Fabiano 1985).

At the first meeting, the staff make it clear that Danny and the other group members can and will be returned to court for re-sentencing if they miss sessions without good reason. They then try to put the group members more at ease, starting with 'warm-up' exercises and going on to show them how to play a video game aimed at encouraging players to question their own values. The group meets twice a week for four months, and Danny attends almost all the sessions and seems to make progress. After the group meetings end, he remains on probation under the supervision of one of the centre's probation officers for a further eight months. This gives her an opportunity to relate what he has learnt during the life of the group to his individual circumstances, and to provide a listening ear when he has difficulties. He has decided to look for a place on a training scheme for gardeners, and she helps him to locate an employer running such a course.

In this case, work on clients' offending behaviour is given priority over extended counselling, although the group uses techniques recognizable to counsellors. Only when the main part of the court order has been satisfactorily completed does one-to-one work begin, and although the probation officer has quite a large caseload of other offenders under her supervision, she has come to know Danny well (for more information on such cognitive group work in practice, see Raynor *et al.* (1994)).

In case illustrations 2.1 and 2.2, the role of probation officers in enforcing court orders is apparent: the probation service has always been an agency of social control, but in crucial respects this aspect of its work has been increased in the 1990s for political reasons (see McLaughlin and Muncie 1994; Beaumont 1995; Ward and Lacey 1995). This has implications for the ethical practice of counselling in such a setting, to which I return in Chapter 4. Nevertheless, all the probation workers mentioned in the two case illustrations drew upon counselling skills in their routine interactions with their clients.

Prison work

Probation officers, as noted in the case illustrations above, also work in prisons. If there are problems applying counselling theories and ethical practices in field probation settings, the reader can imagine how much these are magnified in the prison setting. All the same, counselling is effectively practised inside prisons, and there is considerable potential for more such work, as the following case illustration shows.

Case illustration 2.3

Geoff is serving a prison sentence for his part in an armed robbery. He receives an unexpected request, while working in the prison library, to return to the wing where he lives. He is met by Jackie, the prison's Anglican chaplain, who invites him to come into an empty office and shuts the door behind him. She tells him she wants him to prepare himself for some bad news.

Geoff has no idea what this might be, so he waits in silence. Jackie goes on to say that she is very sorry to have to tell him that his mother has died suddenly in a motorway accident. His father is in hospital, but is expected to make a full recovery. They were on their way to visit him at the prison at about nine o'clock that morning, and another car crossed the central reservation on a dual carriageway outside Coventry and hit their car head on. She has checked to ensure that his sister has been informed. Geoff's mother was taken to the same hospital as his father, and her body is in the chapel there. Jackie asks him if there is anything she can do to help, and whether he smokes. He nods and she offers him a pack of cigarettes and a box of matches. He takes one, lights it and gives her the cigarettes and matches back.

Nothing is said for a few minutes. Eventually, Jackie asks if he would prefer to be alone. Geoff says that he would, at least for the time being. Jackie leaves, waiting in the office opposite. She has a feeling that this will be the first of several sessions with Geoff, and she is glad that she made some telephone calls, checking the details, before sending for Geoff.

Chaplains in the UK have often trained in the clinical theology tradition (Lake 1986), which has a good deal in common with counselling. Although explicitly Christian, pastoral care in clinical theology begins with non-directive listening. Geoff may want to talk about his offending as well as discussing his grief: time will tell. For the moment, Jackie's involvement with him belongs at the listening stage of pastoral care, and she will leave it to him to set the future agenda. If he makes further contact, he will be offered a series of appointments and Jackie will clarify the extent to which he wishes to discuss religious matters, and issues relating to his offending and imprisonment, if at all.

Some offenders do need to discuss their guilty feelings with someone who has the necessary understanding to help them to come to terms with what they have done: 'a Christian sees the recognition of sin not as a counsel of despair but as a ground for hope' (Atherton 1987: 95). Apart from this, chaplains' role in prisons includes a normal pastoral one, ministering to the inmates affiliated to their denomination (and, in the case of Anglicans, to many nominal Christians too). They also have a management function, although they are usually adept at avoiding co-option by the prison service. They have certain regular tasks, such as visiting prisoners in the segregation unit and breaking bad news, as in case illustration 2.3.

These call for a high level of counselling skills, and for formal counselling at times (see Chapters Three, Four and Five).

Prison chaplaincies have responsibility for arranging for the religious needs of all denominations and creeds. Until recently, the Anglican chaplains in some prisons failed to make adequate arrangements in this respect, but the prison service has improved the service to prisoners over the last decade by ensuring that chaplains are aware of their responsibilities, and by publishing information about the requirements of different religions and how these can best be met in the case of prisoners. Nevertheless, some prisons still fail to provide properly for inmates' religious and dietary needs (Dominelli *et al.* 1995).

Although Jackie may not seem to do much in the brief interview with Geoff described above, she prepares carefully for the discussion. She makes it clear that she is available for further sessions, and shows sensitivity based on previous experience and on the literature about how to break bad news (see for example Williams 1991; Buckman 1992). Although kept busy by an enormous potential caseload and the routine duties mentioned above, prison chaplains have a chance to work in some depth with at least a few individuals. This might involve follow-up work with those who have been given bad news, but could equally include supporting individuals who are feeling suicidal, helping others to deal with guilt about their offences, and actually encouraging some prisoners to think about the harm they have done to others. While chaplains work from an explicitly religious value base, their services are used by many imprisoned clients (and by fellow staff) who do not share their beliefs. They are valued for their perceived independence of the prison system and for their familiarity with profound spiritual issues, as well as their counselling skills and practice.

As in the wider community, so in prisons there are opportunities to engage in counselling in multidisciplinary settings, which can influence the practice of a variety of professionals and improve their relationships with clients.

Project illustration 2.1

At a new prison for young offenders, there was considerable concern about the number of vulnerable youths being remanded in custody by local courts. Some were very young and the regime, which had a relatively low level of staff supervision, made it difficult to protect them from bullying. Others were emotionally or mentally unstable, and some were sent to prison only because courts had insufficient information about them to

> make a decision as to whether it was acceptable to grant them bail. The prison replaced two other remand centres which had been notorious for a very high rate of suicides and self-injuries, and the governor was anxious to avoid a repetition of this problem.
>
> He set up a bail information scheme with funding from the prison service. As well as providing accurate information to courts, which enabled them to release many young offenders on bail at their second court appearance, this project provided opportunities for prison officers to try more satisfying kinds of work, and for the prison's probation officers to train them in basic counselling and interviewing skills. Prison officers and probation officers seconded to work on the scheme tried to interview all new inmates in the first few days after they arrived from court. (In most areas, there are now court-based bail information schemes, which try to prevent unnecessary remands into custody in the first place; at the time when most prison-based schemes were established, this network of court schemes was extremely patchy, partly because of opposition by the probation officers' trade union, NAPO, to the establishment of court schemes (see Cameron 1989).)
>
> Interestingly, the young prisoners spoke highly of the listening and helping abilities of the uniformed staff, and some found that when they were interviewed by probation officers (trained social workers), they were given less time to put their case for bail. Most of the prison officers responded very favourably to the opportunity to enhance their job satisfaction, and they also saw the sense in getting as many vulnerable, minor offenders out of prison as possible (Williams 1992a).

This project was an interesting example of a coincidence of interests between two professional groups in a prison setting being turned to practical effect. In the process, relationships between the two groups were improved, as were those between prison officers and inmates, and some basic counselling skills were imparted to staff who traditionally rely on cruder methods of person management (see below).

This approach has a long history in the prison setting. Prison officers have for many years been unhappy with the notion that they are no more than turnkeys, arguing that they should be involved in working with all aspects of prisoners' lives, and recently the prison authorities in England and Wales have responded to this with the 'Better Jobs Initiative'. This aims to improve the quality of working life for main-grade prison officers by giving them opportunities for involvement in specialist projects, and by drawing them all into the process of assessing inmates during sentence planning. Bail information schemes were encouraged to spread under the aegis of this initiative, as was Social Work in Prisons (SWIP).

Project illustration 2.2

Social Work in Prisons involves more systematic and routine joint work by probation officers and uniformed staff, dealing with more intimate problems presented by prisoners (as well as routine 'welfare' work such as chasing up the reasons for family members missing visits to prisoners, or telephoning local-authority departments that have failed to respond to letters from inmates). Not surprisingly, some prisoners resent the involvement of uniformed staff in confidential matters concerning their personal relationships, and prefer to talk to professionally qualified probation officers or psychologists, who do not have the same kind of disciplinary powers as prison officers and are bound by professional ethics to protect personal information. In some prisons, however, the principle of SWIP has been accepted by a majority of inmates, who happily talk to whichever 'SWIP officer' is on duty when they come to the office.

In their routine contact with SWIP schemes, the caring motivation of prison officers has become harder for prisoners to deny: uniformed SWIP officers have gone out of their way to help them, and inmates begin to 'see behind the uniform'. The crude 'us and them' barriers erected on both sides have begun to come down. No doubt this makes prison officers' jobs more complex, but it is also likely to make them more rewarding, and to improve relationships and regimes (Williams 1991; Williams and Eadie 1994). As the members of different professions gain an insight into the problems and culture of those with whom they work, defensive postures become more difficult to sustain (Woodhouse and Pengelly 1991).

The dangers of alienation and cynicism among prison staff have long been recognized, and various job-enrichment strategies have been tried in different countries. In certain circumstances, alienated workers may welcome change, and this can include a commitment on the part of prison officers to greater involvement with prisoners as a way of increasing their own job satisfaction and prestige (Toch and Klofas 1982).

Victim Support

A variety of organizations exists to support the victims of crime. For example, Victim Support itself has a national network of local schemes. Specialist organizations counsel women who have been physically abused or raped. Other, smaller groups have been set up to support, for example, the families of murder victims or the families of people killed by careless drivers.

The degree of involvement with clients varies considerably between and within these different services. For example, many Victim Support cases involve a single visit by a volunteer who gives practical advice and general support. Victims of crime are often grateful for this level of contact and feel the need for nothing more (or they may not have seen the need in the first place, but politely accepted the well meant gesture of a 'cold calling' volunteer). More complex problems may need a much more protracted involvement – and more expertise on the part of the counsellor (see Tyndall 1993).

Case illustration 2.4

Ben and Marie are a young black couple who have recently moved into a new house. They come home from the cinema one night with their young daughter, Louise, to find that their house has been burgled. There is quite a lot of mess and damage, and Louise is distressed to find that her clothes and toys have been disturbed by the intruders. The police are called, and establish that Louise's window had been left open by her father and this provided the means of access. She has nightmares and difficulty sleeping. A few evenings later, a local Victim Support volunteer, Jimmie, comes round.

When they tell their story, he says how sorry he is that they have had such an unpleasant welcome to the area – and tells them about some of the local facilities. They talk about Louise's disturbed nights, and he tells them that this is common. He has a brief word with her, and finds out that she is frightened that the intruders will come back again. He explains that they probably came into the house because there was an easy way to get in, not because of anything she or her father had done or not done, and that such burglaries tend to be opportunist and unplanned. She says that the burglary was her fault, and Marie replies that anyone can forget to shut a window – and that if anyone is to blame, it is her and Ben rather than Louise.

After she has been put to bed, Jimmie explains the statistical probability of a repeat burglary within the next few months, and advises Ben and Marie to see the local crime prevention officer for advice about security. He also offers to come again to help them fit window locks. He says that they should not worry unduly about Louise feeling guilty about the burglary: this a common reaction, however irrational it may seem.

Before his next visit, he talks to the Victim Support scheme's coordinator, who gives him a simple booklet about burglary for Louise (see the examples reproduced as appendices in Victim Support Bedfordshire, undated), and advises him on how to work with her if she remains distressed (drawing upon practice experience and research conducted by a local Victim Support scheme; this is also reported in Victim Support Bedfordshire, undated).

This case involves the possibility of longer-term counselling, but the likelihood is that there will be no need for further intervention after the second visit. Jimmie is a combination of a good neighbour and a voluntary counsellor, but mostly makes one-off visits. He can call upon a rudimentary kind of supervision from the scheme coordinator, but would be hard pressed to offer long-term help to someone traumatized by a serious crime. He has limited time to offer, and there is also a limit to the amount of distress he is personally equipped to cope with. Like many of his fellow volunteers, he is glad to be able to help, but he knows his limitations and he is generally glad when none of his cases is too complicated.

In recent years, Victim Support has begun to provide more sophisticated training for some of its volunteers. It can now assist, for example, the families of people who have been murdered and can provide long-term help to raped women – but only in some parts of the UK. Similarly, there are projects in some inner-city areas to help deal with the effects of racial harassment and abuse (see Chapter One) although there is little official help available for self-help projects aimed at tackling this problem.

There is a world of difference between the straightforward victims of domestic burglary and someone who has been raped. Some Victim Support schemes actually do not work with victims of sexual violence as a matter of policy – but there is not always an alternative local organization to turn to. In this sense, women who have been raped are likely to get a poor service from the criminal justice system for years to come. This is discussed further in Chapter Six, and it is also touched upon in case illustration 2.5.

Case illustration 2.5

Marianne was raped by a work colleague almost a year ago. After discussion with her family, she decided not to report the incident. They felt, and she agreed, that the prosecution of the perpetrator would do nothing to improve her situation, and that the trauma of taking the matter through the courts would make her feel even worse. Since then, she has begun drinking quite heavily, she has given up her job and moved to a less well paid but similar post in another town, and she has found herself being irritable with her partner. She has nightmares about the rape, and sometimes thinks she sees the perpetrator in the street, although when she gets closer she realizes it is not him. These problems are increasingly getting her down, and she telephones the Samaritans. In the course of a lengthy discussion, she is told about the local Rape Crisis centre.

She telephones the centre and is relieved to find herself talking to a woman who has had a broadly similar experience. When she describes how she has been feeling and behaving, the counsellor is able to reassure her that these are normal reactions to what she has been through. She is told about the other services the centre offers in addition to the phoneline, and agrees to meet the counsellor, Lynne, the following evening at the centre.

Lynne has considerable experience of working with rape survivors. (The women's movement has pointed out the unfortunate connotations of the word 'victim' in this context: if a woman who is raped is labelled as a victim, she has little opportunity to alter that status. Rape is an act of violence, often life-threatening, and 'survivor' serves better to describe its seriousness and a sense of the woman as self-determined. This is discussed further by 'T' (1988).) She recognizes some of the symptoms of post-traumatic stress disorder in Marianne's description of her feelings and reactions, and knows that counselling over a period of time is called for in such cases. Unfortunately, the centre can only afford to keep its telephone lines open and staffed for part of the week, and a good deal of voluntary effort is used on fund raising. Whenever the telephones are answered, there are calls like Marianne's. It is hard to get help for callers from anywhere else: most do not want a referral to mental health services, and few can afford private counselling. Lynne feels reasonably confident that she can provide appropriate help to Marianne, but there have been times when she has felt out of her depth in dealing with such cases.

While the research evidence is becoming reasonably clear about the sort of help which is needed by most people with post-traumatic stress disorder (Walker 1990; Brown 1991; Gibson 1991; Hodgkinson and Stewart 1991; Scott and Stradling 1992), more research is required (McFarlane 1994), and appropriate services are not necessarily available. A woman going to her general practitioner with Marianne's account and symptoms might be referred to a psychiatrist, but there could be a long wait and the act of labelling her as having a mental health problem might well exacerbate her suffering, at least in the short term.

There is, however, some disagreement in the literature about this issue. After major disasters, it appears that most referrals for counselling are received through general practitioners (Salter 1990), so it may be that many people do trust their own doctor to interpret and validate the distress they experience after traumatic events. Rape Crisis centres make referrals to mental health services only rarely, preferring to avoid medical labelling. Some research also suggests that, while counselling is helpful, focused cognitive approaches to treatment may be more effective in preventing post-traumatic stress disorder (Foa *et al.* 1991). According to Duckworth (1987), counselling is appropriate but it may need to be more directive than usual in challenging distorted perceptions such as self-blame by victims. Counsellors need to assess the appropriateness of particular approaches for individual clients, bearing in mind the occupational culture of their workplace if this is relevant, and it is particularly difficult to arrive at accurate assessments of this kind in cases of post-traumatic stress (McFarlane 1994). Assessment may need to be a continuing process rather than a matter of initial 'diagnosis'.

Women who have been raped need sensitive support, and they ought to have a choice about whether they go to the police and whether they call upon the resources of the voluntary agencies and the National Health Service. These choices do not presently exist in many areas. Those working with survivors of rape have developed a particular expertise, which should be more widely available. They refer to the particular type of post-traumatic shock experienced by such survivors as rape trauma syndrome (Kendall 1993).

People who have to give evidence in court may need support – and this applies to both victims ánd witnesses. This need is beginning to be met by Victim Support schemes, at least in the higher courts.

Not only the victims of crime and disasters, but also those who help to deal with them, can suffer trauma. The needs of such staff are considered later in this chapter.

COUNSELLING AND THE CONSTRAINTS UNDER WHICH IT IS PRACTISED

From this brief survey of some of the different counselling situations in criminal justice settings, it will be clear that those who do this work, whatever their job titles, face difficult and demanding client needs. We have already begun to see some of the constraints that prevent these workers and volunteers from providing the kind of service they believe to be necessary.

A common, and perhaps unsurprising, theme is the lack of resources for meeting clients' needs. In case illustration 2.1, places in a sex offenders' group are a scarce resource, despite all the limitations of such groups as they currently exist in UK prisons. In case illustration 2.3, the chaplain is constrained by the pressure of other, routine work (and again, this is a problem for other workers in the criminal justice system who are subject to the priorities of their employers as well as to the competing demands and needs of different groups of potential clients). In case illustration 2.4, there is a lack of resources for the ideal level of supervision of volunteers, and in case illustration 2.5 political decisions about resourcing priorities have excluded the needs of survivors of sexual violence from service provision, leaving voluntary organizations to pick up the pieces as best they can. In the long term, such clashes of priorities take their toll on staff morale and indeed diminish counsellors' ability to offer effective help (Halton 1995).

Structural constraints are also a common theme. In case illustration 2.1, the probation officer sees the need for work to be done in the community with an individual, but the judgement about the appropriate level of punishment is made elsewhere. The court decides that punishing the offender is a higher priority than tackling his offending behaviour. The field probation officer's structural role as a community-based worker permits no more than brief involvement, although in this particular case there is effective liaison with prison-based colleagues to ensure continuity (something which does not always happen in practice). Similarly in case illustration 2.4, the role of the volunteer is limited by his relatively brief training and by time constraints: he has volunteered to work for a few hours each week as a 'good neighbour', not to engage in long-term counselling. He may not have the knowledge or resources to make appropriate referrals in cases where longer-term counselling is needed.

The criminal justice setting itself can hinder constructive engagement. Because counselling is not the dominant paradigm, issues can be ignored, as is likely to happen in case illustration 2.1 where in the prison environment security commands a high level of resources but treatment does not, so that many offenders whose behaviour should be addressed are not engaged in treatment. Prison is also an obvious example of the setting as a constraint in itself: prisoners may find it hard to discuss sensitive issues with staff who have disciplinary functions as well as helping roles, or it may be simply unsafe for prisoners to talk about their offences. In case illustration 2.2 also, the setting and the court order are in danger of getting in the way of the work that needs to be done: the group workers have to be clear about their powers over clients and the compulsory nature of the involvement, and this has to be handled carefully if it is not to interfere with the formation of effective helping relationships (see Earnshaw 1993; Senior 1993b; Williams 1995a). Again, in case illustration 2.5, institutional arrangements may make counselling inaccessible to those in need: a woman who has been raped is unlikely to see her problem as a psychiatric one, and thereby misses the opportunity of entering counselling.

These issues are all addressed further in Chapters Four and Six. What is clear from the discussion above is that the place of counselling is somewhat marginal in criminal justice settings, despite its evident importance in terms of client need.

THE STATUS OF COUNSELLORS AND COUNSELLING IN DIFFERENT SETTINGS

Counselling is marginalized in criminal justice settings partly because of the strong occupational cultures of the police and the prison service, partly because of the politics of criminal justice in the UK in recent years, and also because of the structural factors outlined earlier. Nevertheless, there are instances where the need for counselling is generally recognized and where those with the necessary counselling experience are accorded high status within the organizations concerned.

The police and the prison service in the UK have traditionally been hierarchical, male-dominated, culturally homogeneous organizations. They have each evolved a macho, quasi-military 'canteen culture', in which any perceived weakness in an individual is seen as a threat to the strength and solidarity of the organization (Lombardo 1981, 1985; Holdaway 1983; Duckworth 1988; Fielding 1988, 1994; Sim 1994). Black people are regarded with suspicion, if not with outright hostility (Pearson *et al.* 1989), and women are confined to traditional 'feminine' roles wherever possible (Fielding

1994; Horn 1995). In this atmosphere, concern for the welfare of offenders or even for the victims of disasters can come to be regarded with suspicion – and welfare needs of staff themselves are equated with weakness (Reeves 1995; McKenzie 1987; Zimmer 1987; Gibson 1991; Hodgkinson and Stewart 1991). The total picture is more complex than this suggests, though. Women and black people are entering the prison and police services in increasing numbers, and the involvement of the police in particular in large-scale disasters has led to greater understanding of the need for staff counselling (Scott and Stradling 1992).

There is disturbing evidence, however, that in the uniformed services the response to disasters was not always a constructive one in terms of supporting staff suffering from traumatic stress: according to Salter (1990: 320), who was involved as a psychologist in the aftermath of the Lockerbie disaster, 'despite the expressed concern, there has been a strong reluctance to implement even the most minor of changes'. This has changed, with greater organizational awareness of the costs of allowing staff stress to go untreated. This may be partly due to increased concern with the financial cost of losing expensively trained staff, but it has had the effect of improving service provision (Salter 1995).

Where psychologists have been present at the scene of disasters to support members of the uniformed services, they have sometimes been perceived as management spies, although there is clear research evidence that counselling fairly soon after traumatic events can reduce the number of people suffering post-traumatic stress (Hodgkinson and Stewart 1991). This cynicism is part of the reaction to disasters by the staff involved; they find that everything they had taken for granted is called into question, and the inability of what seemed like an all-powerful agency such as the police to protect its staff is a disturbing reminder of their vulnerability (Salter 1995).

Awareness of the need for post-traumatic stress counselling has spread, albeit to a limited extent, to other criminal justice agencies. Prison officers, for example, are now referred for counselling after direct involvement in prisoners' suicides (Liebling 1995), and some social services departments have introduced staff counselling schemes (Gibson 1991). So, too, have many other large employers. McLeod and Cooper (1992), for example, found that most fire brigades had some staff counselling provision as part of their stress management strategies. The larger banks and building societies, recognizing the likelihood that staff may be present during armed robberies, have a system of staff training as well as providing post-incident counselling

(Richards 1994). The British Post Office has developed a system of post-incident debriefing for groups of staff exposed to traumatic incidents, with provision for trauma counselling in appropriate cases (Tehrani and Westlake 1994), and British Airways has made similar arrangements. Some social services departments have learnt from the experience of large-scale disasters over the last two decades, and have set up proactive arrangements whereby trained workers and volunteers from agencies like Cruse Bereavement Care and the Samaritans are ready to respond in the event of future disasters (Hodgkinson and Stewart 1991). This is a front-line response aimed at helping people through the immediate period of crisis and ensuring that those in need are referred for specialist counselling.

Recognizing that many types of employment are potentially stressful, some employers are now routinely carrying out stress audits (Cooper and Cartwright 1994). These may indicate a need for the provision of counselling, or for short-term problem-solving exercises in specific circumstances, or indeed for both (Duckworth 1988).

The policy dimension

Alongside the 'new right' penal policies, which have increased the prison population in England and Wales and made prison the centre of the criminal justice system, there is a widespread understanding among those who work in the system that punishment alone will not change offenders' behaviour. This has provided opportunities to advance counselling as part of the solution: thus, the Sex Offender Treatment Programme, for all its flaws, brings psychologists, probation officers and prison officers together in interdisciplinary group work. Prison officers have come to see involvement in offender counselling as a way of enhancing their own job satisfaction and status, as project illustrations 2.1 and 2.2 have shown (see also Williams 1996). Similarly, outside prison, psychiatrists and psychologists are working alongside probation staff to engage with groups of sexual offenders in offence-focused counselling. Such counselling is also gaining credibility in work with other types of offenders, as we shall see in the next chapter.

Unfortunately, the criminal justice system has become a political battleground in Britain, and politicians have taken to decrying the efforts of the probation service and deriding its links with social work. In one sense, this does not augur well for counselling-based approaches to work with offenders – but probation officers have shown signs, however reluctantly, of engaging in the battle to retain the values and methods of counselling and social work in their professional repertoire (Nellis 1995; Williams 1995a). Initial training for probation officers has been increasingly competence based, emphasizing outcomes rather than processes (Hayman 1993), and this has moved it away from detailed attention to processes and ways of relating to people. Individuals are increasingly undertaking specialist training (for example in bereavement counselling), recognizing that more than pre-specified competences are needed to give clients an appropriate service. It may be that, ultimately, counselling and its values cannot coexist with punitive and simplistic political approaches to criminal justice policy, but criminal justice professionals have shown themselves to be inventive in defending their values, both overtly and covertly.

Where Victim Support is concerned, there has always been a recognition that the 'good neighbour' approach has its limitations, and that some crime victims will need more specialized support. For example, where a family member has been murdered, grieving tends to take longer than after a natural death (Newburn 1993), and under the Victim's Charter (Home Office 1990) both the probation service and Victim Support schemes have an important role (Brown *et al.* 1990; Johnston 1994, 1995). In some areas, probation staff have been specially trained to work with victims' families (as in West Yorkshire: see Johnston 1994, 1995). Elsewhere, this is in its infancy, but Victim Support volunteers are working with probation officers to support families (for example in Merseyside: see Aubrey and Hossack 1994). Clearly, there is a good deal of development work still to be done, but the high level of satisfaction with counselling provided to crime victims in Australia under 'victims' rights' legislation points the way forward (Wilkie *et al.* 1992). People who have experienced victimization are generally quick to see the benefits of victim support counselling, although in many cases this need be only short term and will mainly involve listening and practical help.

In some probation areas, a partnership with victim agencies is envisaged as a routine part of work with life-sentence prisoners. One area, for example:

> has a policy of involvement with lifer cases at the earliest opportunity following arrest. This will be the appropriate point for victim issues to be considered and wherever necessary they will become an integral part of the Probation Service's work thereafter, sometimes in partnership with a victims' organisation.
> (Northumbria Probation Service 1993: 3)

This policy seems likely to have considerable resource implications, and it is unclear to what extent these have been considered – or how routinely the policy has been implemented, since it is a fairly new one. It seems to apply only to newly sentenced lifers.

Research (Johnston 1994) suggests that West Yorkshire and Northumbria represent one extreme of a continuum. While probation areas such as these are clearly willing to invest considerable resources in the provision of services to victims of crime, probation managers in other areas (including some metropolitan areas) have taken the opposite view. At least two probation areas refuse to initiate any enquiries about victims, as suggested in the Victim's Charter (Kosh and Williams 1995).

In many rural areas, the model of work advocated by the proponents of the West Yorkshire scheme would be impossible to fund and resource fully. Johnston's enquiries have established that a variety of alternative ways of complying with the Victim's Charter are emerging. In two rural areas, for example, a small number of probation officers receive special training and undertake Victim's Charter work on behalf of their colleagues. Another probation service has had discussions with local Victim Support schemes about ways of 'contracting out' such work in a formal partnership, using the grant-giving powers in the Criminal Justice Act 1991 (Johnston 1994).

Politically, victim support agencies are in a delicate position. In the UK, Victim Support itself has been careful to avoid overt intervention in political debates about criminal justice, and the evidence is that most victims of crime individually prefer to avoid undue involvement in judicial decision making – although they want to be kept informed (Reeves 1995; Reeves and Wright 1995). Focusing narrowly upon the treatment of victims of crime, however, Victim Support has discreetly lobbied the government about specific issues such as the mechanisms for providing victims with information and for financial compensation. Despite its apolitical stance, Victim Support nationally operates as an effective campaigning organization in certain circumstances; for example, when the Home Secretary announced cuts in the compensation scheme for criminal injuries in 1994, considerable embarrassment on the government's part was generated by Victim Support's press releases, conference speeches, and so on.

For the most part, however, the apolitical posture is maintained. In practice, this is itself a political position, and it has proved to be an astute one: in 1993, at a time of severe financial restraint, the Home Office increased funding for Victim Support by 20 per cent.

To be fair, however, the political restraint exercised by the staff and volunteers of Victim Support schemes in the UK has been important in other respects. In the USA, victims of crime have been used as a political football, and increasingly harsh measures have been taken against offenders in the name of victims without anything significant being done to improve the circumstances of the victims (Elias 1993).

The mainstream victim support agencies' work is complemented by (or sometimes in competition with) that of groups working with victims of particular types of crime. For example, Rape Crisis and Women's Aid have sometimes assisted with the training of Victim Support volunteers, and all three organizations refer clients to each other. There is potential for conflict over resourcing: the police and some local authorities tend to see Victim Support groups as more 'respectable' than the other agencies, which are explicit about the feminist commitment of their staff and volunteers, and the police have a good deal of power where victims of crime are concerned.

It appears that to a large extent, the place of counselling in criminal justice agencies in the UK is peripheral and insecure – but that substantial inroads are being made, and that some projects in other English-speaking countries are leading their criminal justice systems to value counselling more than in the past.

The scope for professional conflicts

In the case illustrations in this chapter, some potential conflicts of values for the counsellors were touched upon. Probation officers may see a need for counselling, and try to make a case for it in the court setting, but be thwarted by sentencers' differing priorities. If the magistrates or judge decide in a particular case that the need for punishment or public protection overrides the offender's needs, their view quite properly prevails. But the issue is not always so clear cut.

The difficult obligations that can accompany the counselling role are illustrated by a case study in a recent book (Dominelli *et al.* 1995). In the example given, a probation officer discovers that there are disparities between the way black and white defendants are sentenced for apparently similar offences in the local magistrates' court. He draws the evidence in a number of recent sentencing decisions to the attention of the clerk to the justices, who is responsible for magistrates' training and for advising them on the law. The clerk argues that each decision was taken on the merits of the individual case, and that in any event the local magistrates are about to receive training on 'race awareness'. Meanwhile, the probation officer is advised by senior staff that the matter should be allowed to drop – and that future correspondence with the court should be cleared with the management before it is sent.

While counsellors have a responsibility to confront injustices revealed by their practice, there are limitations upon how effectively this can be done by those working in the criminal justice system. The worker in the case study risks disciplinary action if he continues to 'make waves' – and black staff in particular are frequently the subject of such procedures. In courts and in prisons, there are risks attached to 'whistle blowing'. This is not to say that it should not be attempted in serious cases of injustice, but an appeal to the values of counselling is unlikely to receive a very sympathetic hearing. Such complaints need to be framed in the dominant discourse (in this case, that of formal justice), even though prompted by the worker's adherence to the values and principles of counselling, and this can be a very difficult balancing act for individual workers to perform. As the case study suggests, the role of line managers in promoting professional values is crucial.

Value conflicts between counsellors in criminal justice agencies and their employers are increasingly likely in a political climate in which politicians have been questioning the whole ethical basis of probation work and imposing managerialist policies upon all the services concerned (see Chapter Five). These trends inevitably set up conflicts between service managers, who try to adapt to a changing political environment, and front-line workers who are dealing with the consequences of national policies as they affect their clients. There is a danger that such conflicts can lead to a polarization, whereby the managers begin to see professional staff as 'part of the problem rather than as part of the solution' (McLaughlin and Muncie 1994: 120; see also Beaumont 1995). This issue will be discussed further in Chapter Six, and case illustration 2.6 also raises some of the pertinent issues.

Case illustration 2.6

As part of his regular supervision session with his senior probation officer, Mark has brought the case of Delroy for discussion. Mark wrote a court report about Delroy, proposing that he be placed on probation, but in the event he received a short prison sentence. He is about to be released, and will have nowhere to live. Mark is newly qualified, and does not know the area very well: he is seeking information and advice about local housing agencies. His senior officer tells him that service policy is not to offer voluntary aftercare to prisoners serving less than 12-month sentences. There is no legal obligation to assist such short-term prisoners on their release.

Mark objects, saying that Delroy is highly likely to get into further trouble if he is not given some support when he comes out of prison. The senior probation officer insists that there is no way Mark can get involved in doing this work: there are simply not enough resources for voluntary aftercare cases to be allocated to probation officers, and the duty officer will see Delroy if he comes to the office.

Legally and managerially, the senior is quite right: since 1992, the probation service has not been obliged to offer through-care to short-sentence prisoners during or after their sentences. Professionally, Mark may have the stronger argument: homelessness is highly likely to lead to further offending, and practical help is often the best way to engage in more offence-focused work with ex-prisoners. Once a client's trust has been gained by giving assistance with what he defines as his immediate problem, there is more scope for discussion of other, agency-defined priorities. Ethically, there is an issue about whether it is right to deny a service to vulnerable clients. In all areas of statutory social work, there is a tension of this kind: 'Preventive measures, which would be more effective and more economical in the long run, are all too often given low priority in favour of a patching-up response' (Brearley 1995: 47). In the context of prisoner through-care, practitioners and academics have been pointing this out for nearly 30 years (Parris 1968; Monger *et al.* 1981; Corden and Clifton 1983; Hicks 1986; Williams 1991, 1995a).

Breaking bad news

Prisons do not make it easy for counsellors to practise in sensitive and professional ways, but it is nevertheless possible to do so despite the constraints imposed by the penal setting. For example, prison psychologists have built up considerable experience of working effectively with clients who are HIV positive.

Case illustration 2.7

Mike is a prison psychologist, and he has received the results of an HIV test on David, with whom he has been working for some weeks. David came to him worried that he might have contracted AIDS, and they spent some time discussing the pros and cons of having the test, and its limitations, as well as the ways in which the HIV virus is transmitted. Eventually David had decided to go ahead, and now Mike has to break the news that the result is positive. He delivers a note to the wing asking to see David that afternoon when he gets back from his education class.

David arrives soon afterwards, clearly agitated. Mike gives him a cup of tea, closes the office door and unplugs the telephone. He gently tells David the result and they discuss the implications. They talk for a long time, and Mike makes it clear that he feels they need further discussion later in the day – and subsequently. He offers to get David a copy of a chapter from a recent book about the HIV virus and some leaflets for prisoners supplied by the Terrence Higgins Trust, and agrees to arrange for him to meet the counsellor from the local group of Body Positive when she visits the prison later in the week. They discuss how David will tell his partner the test result, and Mike agrees to sit in at the beginning of the visit, as well as finding out what support groups exist in David's home town. He checks whether he has David's consent to discuss the diagnosis with the prison chaplain and probation officer, and they talk about the implications of sharing the information. He begins to feel that David is handling the news quite well, but checks this perception with him before arranging a time to meet again in order to agree a programme for their future work together. Finally, he makes sure that David will not be isolated if he needs to talk to someone when he goes back to his wing.

Because of the anxiety in our culture about discussing death, the task of helping people come to terms with a potentially fatal medical diagnosis is given to specialists, whether they be medical, psychological or religious by training (see Machin 1990; Ussher 1990). David is well and is reasonably likely to remain so, but he needs to consider the worst possible implications of his HIV-positive status and come to terms with them. His partner also needs support. The taboo against talking about death can be broken within a professional relationship, and it is obviously important that this is done in a supportive and well informed way. In cases where the client is dying, this kind of help can enable him or her to come to terms with it and to make the most of the coming months or years. Some counsellors report that in many cases

> the fear and uncertainty were replaced by resignation, then tranquillity and acceptance, in a way which provided both

> inspiration and hope to all of those associated with the dying person. Each death . . . was accompanied by a sense of peace and resolution, regardless of the physical and psychological difficulties which had accompanied the preceding illness.
> (Ussher 1990: 287)

This kind of positive resolution will be much more difficult to achieve in prison, where the climate is a coercive one, and careful preparation will be needed. Even seriously ill prisoners, if they are classified as meriting high-security conditions, will not be released to die in a hospice until a very late stage. All the arrangements are complicated by the prejudice and fear surrounding AIDS, and anyone dying in prison has to be the subject of a coroner's inquest, which delays funerals. It has to be said, however, that, sadly, prisons are becoming more experienced in dealing with these sorts of issues, and their practice is gradually improving as a result (Curran 1987; Padel *et al.* 1992; Padel 1995).

Counsellors working for the first time with people who are dying tend to be very worried about whether they will be able to help, and many expect it to be a depressing experience. Where there is no proper support in dealing with the pain and distress such work arouses in the counsellor, this may well be the case, and burn-out can result (Ussher 1990). But some counsellors speak of sharing the last weeks of the life of a dying client as an enormous privilege, and one which makes them feel very fulfilled.

On the practical level, it is clearly important, when working with an issue which generates so much anxiety and feeds to such a large extent upon homophobia and other prejudices, to get one's facts right. A good deal of work has been done by those working in and with prisons to ensure that accurate information is made available in an accessible form to staff and prisoners, and counsellors need to be armed with this material (see Padel *et al.* (1992) for details of the resources available).

SUMMARY

This chapter has outlined some of the locations in which counselling is used in penal and community settings in criminal justice. Probation workers, prison staff and those involved in supporting victims of crime all include counsellors. Counselling may have been marginalized in each of these areas, but it is nonetheless practised and found useful. In each setting, there are ethical and practical constraints upon counsellors and upon other staff who employ counselling skills in their work, but these are overcome in clients' interests. Some of these obstacles to appropriate counselling practice are discussed in depth in Chapters Four and Six. First, Chapter Three examines a number of professional concerns which apply to the practice of counselling in all settings, and pays particular attention to the relevance of race and gender issues for counsellors in criminal justice agencies. It also considers the question of balancing care and control in penal and court-ordered counselling, and looks at some of the constraints upon professional autonomy and confidentiality imposed by the criminal justice context.

This chapter has illustrated the uses of counselling in the criminal justice system, and the next shows how that context limits what counsellors can do in practice – and how it also serves to highlight some problems common to counselling in all settings.

· THREE ·

The practice of counselling in criminal justice

This chapter looks at the ways in which some of the issues common to counselling in any setting are handled specifically in the criminal justice context. While that context may impose limitations upon counsellors and upon the exercise of counselling skills, it also provides a wide variety of opportunities to engage constructively with offenders and with victims of crime. There are considerable similarities and overlaps between some criminal justice settings and social work agencies, and this chapter might be read in conjunction with Judith Brearley's (1995) companion volume in this series, *Counselling and Social Work.*

COUNSELLING, BEFRIENDING OR CONTROLLING?

The probation service has traditionally been expected (in the words of the legislation under which it was established in 1907) to 'advise, assist and befriend' the offenders under its supervision. Since 1991, this duty has been partly superseded by an obligation to provide 'punishment in the community'. This raises a number of complex ethical dilemmas for practitioners, which are considered further in Chapter Four. Some of the tasks which might in future be required of probation officers sit uneasily with their values as social workers and as counsellors – which is one of the reasons this value base is under political attack.

Commercial security staff administered electronic tagging of offenders in the UK because probation officers made it clear that they would not be willing to do so. Prison officers are required to compel inmates to undergo urine tests as part of the 'war on drugs', and so far it has not been proposed that this be undertaken by social workers or probation officers in respect of offenders being supervised in the community (although it happens routinely in the USA and Canada). Probation officers in England and Wales refused to collect ethnic data on people under their supervision until the categories and safeguards had been agreed with black organizations. Social workers in Nazi Germany, however, provided information about members of racial minorities and developed typologies of 'educability' and 'parasitism', which facilitated the classification of alcoholics, people with mental illness and people with disabilities, who were subsequently sent to concentration camps (Lorenz 1994). The power which goes with the counselling role in criminal justice agencies must be used responsibly and accountably. If it is not, counsellors' legitimacy in the eyes of clients can be abused for political ends.

Social workers and probation officers have always been uncomfortable about politically inspired suggestions that they should work in more controlling ways. This is not, as some observers have suggested (for example Sheldon 1995), because they are unaware of the control that has always been inherent in supervising offenders, and neither is it due to a sentimental desire to be 'nice to people'. Clients are well aware of the tension between care and control, and of the power involved in the supervisory relationship. They can tell the difference between control exercised for its own sake, which is an abuse of power, and the control that is necessarily and properly involved in supervision. When politicians impose coercive powers on staff who work with offenders, they threaten the delicate balance that the profession has striven to maintain. Supervisory relationships need to be based upon workers' genuineness and empathy, not solely on vigilance and surveillance.

Befriending was seen, in the early days of the probation service, as a way to gain clients' trust in order to facilitate other types of work. While many probation officers would defend this notion in general terms as part of the social work ethos of the service, befriending might be regarded as rather manipulative if it is done as a means to another end that is not disclosed to the client. What is important, and should not be lost amid the debate about how to deliver 'punishment in the community', is the belief that social work with offenders is based upon unconditional acceptance of clients as people. The police court missionaries used to say, 'Love the sinner, hate the sin'. This has a judgemental ring today, but it makes an important point: it is possible to form professional relationships with people who have committed appalling offences. The purpose of doing so is offence related, as it always was, but this purpose should not be concealed. Indeed, if probation officers are to undertake effective counselling with offenders, it must not be. In making contracts with individual clients, the boundaries of the professional relationship need to be fully discussed.

If clients need befriending and find because of their circumstances that they do 'not always have easy access to friends' (Brearley 1995: 52), the probation service has access to a variety of organizations that can assist. Probation recruits its own volunteers (sometimes called voluntary associates or VAs). In some areas, this task is delegated to the Society of Voluntary Associates (SOVA), which has a national programme of recruitment and training. Specialist organizations befriend (and in some cases also counsel) people with specific types of problems; for example, Cruse helps the bereaved, Samaritans the suicidal, Alcoholics Anonymous and its offshoots the drug misuser, and so on. It is important that such referrals are made in appropriate cases: professional staff could not hope to undertake all the befriending work, and it would not be appropriate for them to do so.

COUNSELLING OR CONFRONTATION?

The environments in which counselling skills are employed within the criminal justice system are not always conducive to a genuinely supportive way of working. This raises the question of whether counselling in its proper sense is actually possible in some of these settings. How, for example, does a counsellor ensure privacy or confidentiality when working in a prison? These issues inevitably recur throughout this book, concerned as it is with the possibilities and limitations of counselling within criminal justice.

The organizational settings in which counselling takes place also impose constraints upon the styles of work employed. For example, emphasis has moved away from attempts at rehabilitation of individual offenders in the prison and probation services in North America and in England and Wales. Instead, political rhetoric emphasizes the need to 'challenge' and 'confront' offending, and professional practice tries to respond. Such terminology suggests a more confrontational style of working than most counsellors feel comfortable with. Some of the issues this raises for practice are discussed in Chapters Four and Five.

THE LIMITS OF PROFESSIONAL AUTONOMY

There will always be limitations on the autonomy of those undertaking counselling in criminal justice settings, as in any other setting, but particular issues affect work in criminal justice agencies. These arise most obviously in cases where counselling is not the primary function of the agency. In his study of the occupational socialization of police officers, Fielding (1988: 21) notes that many new recruits' accounts of their motives for joining the police are 'more redolent of counselling than control'. They want to help people and act as an example, advising on legal matters and serving a community as well as enforcing the law. Only when they gain experience do they realize how little valued the helping, advising and service approaches to policing are within the occupational culture.

Some experienced police officers liken beat policing to social work. They do so in a positive way, believing that this is a necessary part of the job and one which improves relationships with the public, but many are keen to get into specialist work, where promotion prospects are better. Real counselling (such as breaking and dealing with the consequences of bad news, dealing with domestic disputes and helping abused children and raped women to frame their allegations) is, all too often, seen as a role best carried out by women police officers. They are likely to do it better, but that is not why they are given this kind of work: it has a lower status within the police subculture of male aggression, and so becomes 'women's work'. This perception, and the decisions arising from it, obviously do little for the status of counselling or of women within the service. However, the role of outside counsellors in helping with occupational stress and post-traumatic reactions has recently increased, as in the aftermath of disasters such as Lockerbie. This trend may do something to improve police perceptions of counselling (see Chapter Two).

Structured counselling is rarely, if ever, undertaken by the police, although they do frequently come into contact with people who may need it. Some officers work in specialist units alongside social workers, Rape Crisis counsellors, Victim Support staff and others better qualified to assess such needs. Others may have access to specialist staff such as psychologists and psychiatrists. It is clearly important that police officers working with survivors of sexual abuse, spousal assault and rape know how to refer people for counselling and how to decide which cases demand attention of this kind.

Similarly, the role of the police is not normally seen as one of befriending their 'clients'. Although some police officers do befriend people with whom they have worked, this is not really their job. There are usually clear procedures for referring crime victims to local Women's Aid, Samaritans or Victim Support schemes, which befriend in a systematic way.

CONFIDENTIALITY

Voluntary and private counselling agencies lay down strict policies about confidentiality of client information (see Tyndall (1993) for case examples and a discussion of the legal limitations of client confidentiality in such settings). Statutory organizations should be just as rigorous about protecting confidential information, but their other duties restrict the extent to which they can treat confidentiality as sacrosanct. Once again, the degree to which counselling is central to the functions of the agency influences the extent to which its values are upheld. For example:

> When a counselling service for women is one aspect of an organization's function, it takes place in a context where the predominant professional outlook is likely to be different. There are considerable implications and many potential conflicts of ideology when counselling occurs in a setting predominantly geared to either education or social work.
>
> (Perry 1993: 42)

Among the organizations discussed by Perry were Rape Crisis centres, which treat all dealings with their clients as confidential. They may not even know some clients' names. If the police were to approach them for information or evidence, Rape Crisis counsellors would be extremely circumspect. The client's trust in the agency is more important to these counsellors than an easy relationship with the police ('T' (1988) discusses the reasons for this). In rare cases, with the client's active involvement and consent, information is provided in order to assist police enquiries, but this is exceptional. Rape Crisis centres keep few written records, and these are destroyed after a year or so.

Client records kept by statutory agencies are also confidential, at least in theory. But, in practice, if the police make enquiries about probation clients, they will often be given the information they seek. This is particularly true when serious offences are under investigation. Material from probation files on individuals is often photocopied and sent to other criminal justice agencies (rarely to the police, but routinely to prisons, social workers and psychiatrists). These informal exchanges of information occur from time to time, and the police have legal powers under the Police and Criminal Evidence Act 1984 to obtain access to most agency records if such informal requests are denied, although these legal powers have rarely been used.

In these circumstances, a probation client who had been raped but did not want to consider reporting the offence would be well advised to think carefully before discussing it with her probation officer. The probation officer might feel duty bound to discuss with her whether the matter should be reported, and would keep a record of the discussion, which could find its way to other criminal justice agencies.

It has frequently been alleged that prison officers sometimes deliberately disclose the nature of certain offenders' crimes (for example, in the case of those who have harmed children) and that by doing so they deliberately allow other prisoners to mete out rough justice (Priestley (1981) gives many examples; see also O'Dwyer and Carlen (1985) for an example from a women's prison). While these are extreme cases, they illustrate the extent to which different agencies working with offenders vary in their treatment of client confidentiality. Social workers and probation officers cannot guarantee to protect information that relates, for example, to serious criminal offences, or involves a threat to the safety of children. Counsellors in voluntary settings also have ethical problems about concealing such information, but they have more choice. These discrepancies are discussed further in Chapter Five. The cultural differences between the organizations involved, along with the degree of influence counselling and its ideology has in those agencies, are crucial factors in the extent to which client confidentiality is respected. Where counsellors are committed to an individual model of confidentiality, other professionals using counselling skills espouse an 'integrated' model, which allows the sharing of information within a team or agency (Bond 1992; Thomas 1995).

Apart from constraints arising from agency functions, there are other contrasts between voluntary and statutory agencies in respect of confidentiality. Recording practices differ enormously: social workers, probation officers and workers in agencies funded by the probation and social services are likely to keep comprehensive case notes. This can cause complications for the clients of statutory agencies. For example, probation officers realized, in the 1980s, that they were increasing the stigmatization of people with HIV and AIDS by mentioning the medical condition in court reports. To avoid this, they had to devise new ways of getting such information to magistrates – when it was relevant – without inadvertently releasing it to the press or to prisons (see Padel 1995). This illustrated the loose definition of confidentiality that had been applied to reports prepared for courts (and most probation services subsequently added warnings to the front page of reports, advising readers of the client's right to expect the report's confidentiality to be respected).

Voluntary agencies working with HIV-positive people do not need to keep records of this kind. Now that prisoners have some choice (however limited) about sources of advice on HIV infection, it is hardly surprising that many prefer to talk to independent counsellors and those from outside voluntary agencies rather than to the prison's psychologist or probation officer. They can expect a higher respect for confidentiality from the community agency, and probably also a more informal and empathic service. Some prisoners with HIV, significantly, did not even define prison psychologists as counsellors when they were questioned about the services available to them (Miller and Curran 1994).

On the other hand, statutory agencies have one advantage from the client's point of view: they are obliged in some circumstances to make personal records available to their subjects for checking. This safeguard is an important one, although it is little used. Some of the issues it raises are discussed by Brearley (1995: 101–3). There is no reason in principle why voluntary agencies should not extend similar rights to their clients, and some have done so without waiting for legislation. These include the National Association for the Care and Resettlement of Offenders (NACRO 1993), which allows tenants of its housing projects access to their personal files and lets them know that they can correct any inaccuracies they find. The Family Service Unit (1985) has had a comprehensive client access policy since the early days of the legislation affecting statutory agencies. There is, however, some evidence that voluntary agencies have abused the arrangements for checking the criminal records of potential volunteers (Hebenton and Thomas 1993).

Confidentiality is a vital part of the counselling relationship because treating sensitive information with care shows respect for the client. This is part of the process of building a relationship, not least because it provides evidence of the counsellor's understanding of the delicacy of the matters under discussion. Until the client can trust the worker not to abuse confidences, there is little chance of developing a fruitful professional relationship.

Where there are limitations upon the agency's ability to protect confidential information, these should be disclosed at the outset.

Probation officers preparing court reports, for example, should discuss the meaning of confidentiality in that context at the beginning of every piece of work with a new client. Before clients share sensitive personal information, they need to know who is going to have access to it. Court reports are likely to be seen by the defendant's solicitor, the clerk to the court, and the magistrates or judge in all cases. Where younger defendants are concerned, parents have a right to see the reports. If the offender is sent to an attendance centre, the person in charge (usually a police officer) will get a copy of the court report. Where people are imprisoned, the report is sent to the prison and may be seen by administrative and disciplinary staff as well as chaplains, psychologists and anyone else who looks at the file. In serious cases, reports will also be made available to Home Office civil servants and ministers, and to members of panels making decisions about early release.

One would not necessarily want probation officers to go into this degree of detail – nobody would ever tell them anything! But clients have a right to know what records are being kept on them, and who has access to agency files. Most probation services now produce leaflets outlining this information, and these should be given and explained to clients at the earliest opportunity.

The difficulties of protecting confidential information are compounded when agencies work together with each other and share information, both formally and informally. The example above, of prison officers' access to probation reports, illustrates this. While many clients would understand and accept that confidentiality extends beyond the individual worker to include professional colleagues, the community of people with whom confidences are shared has been getting larger. In many areas of work, inter-agency partnerships mean that the criminal justice system as a whole has been greatly enlarged, to include a wide variety of community groups and private companies. The implications for confidentiality have not really been addressed (Thomas (1988 and 1995) and Brearley (1995) consider how this affects social services departments). The notion of client information being confidential between them and the counsellor, and of the counsellor protecting such information from being disclosed to colleagues and co-workers, is central to counselling practice. This is one of the main differences between counselling and the use of counselling skills in criminal justice and other agencies, and the distinction is important. It should be made explicit to clients.

There are ethical dilemmas for counsellors working with offenders that arise less frequently with other client groups. How does one deal with ambiguous information suggesting that a child is being abused, or a serious crime contemplated? The scenario in the film *The Priest*, in which a young girl reveals in the confessional that her father is sexually abusing her, is not as far fetched as some might think. The young priest agonizes about whether he can breach the sacred trust of the confessional to protect a vulnerable child. The girl's father, knowing the rules, tells him to mind his own business. Analogous conditions arise in the course of counselling practice with some regularity, and there are no simple, cut and dried rules on how to deal with them.

As Tyndall (1993: 53) has pointed out, people's motives for making shocking revelations are not always simple or pure. He notes that:

> publicity about a sensational case in the media may give rise to fears and fantasies in clients' minds. At the time when the Yorkshire Ripper was being hunted, marriage guidance counsellors heard many a woman confide that her husband was he. Clients' allegations must be treated seriously but with caution.

Case illustration 3.1

Janine is an independent counsellor working with Mike, a client who has recently been released from prison after serving a long sentence for sexual offences against his stepdaughter. He has been 'born again' during his time in prison, and now says that his religion will prevent him from ever reoffending. He mentions to Janine during a counselling session that he has been taking a neighbour's children swimming at the local pool fairly often during the recent spell of warm weather.

Knowing something of the treatment Mike received from a prison psychologist after participating in a sexual offenders' group during his sentence, Janine regards this disclosure as a warning sign. She says so to Mike and he refuses to discuss the matter any further. Their initial contract included a reference to Mike's parole licence conditions and possible contact between Janine and his probation officer. She is unsure whether to prejudice her good relationship with Mike by ringing the probation officer, and continues the interview without resolving the matter.

Later, in supervision, she discusses the case without disclosing Mike's identity. She decides that her duty to protect potential victims of abuse outweighs the duty to protect Mike's confidentiality, and she telephones the probation officer. When she later tells Mike this, he is furious, and declines to continue seeing Janine. The probation officer reports him to the Home

Office for breaching his parole conditions and he is eventually arrested and returned to prison.

Arrangements are made for him to see a psychologist regularly during his resumed prison sentence, and he makes good progress and is released again under supervision. He is extremely angry about his recall to prison, and this forms a large part of the discussion with his new probation officer.

This case illustration demonstrates the difficulties which can arise when there is a lack of liaison between counsellors and other staff. Janine's initial contract with Mike may not have been sufficiently explicit where the limits of confidentiality were concerned. This could have been remedied if Janine had been able to decide during her penultimate interview with Mike that her obligations towards potential victims were more pressing than those of confidentiality – but this is never an easy or clear decision to make.

Although the law about adult sexual contact with children is unambiguous, the therapeutic relationship that involves legal issues is highly complex and can be extremely ambiguous (Bolton and Bolton 1990). While it is good practice to warn individuals and groups that disclosure of offences may result in the therapist reporting the matter, the case of Mike is not so straightforward. Janine's disclosure of what may be an innocent situation leads directly to Mike going back to prison. She has, however, behaved properly and professionally. Her decision was taken after careful discussion in supervision, and she weighed one risk against another (R. J. Kelly 1990; Meier and Davis 1993). Sexual offenders are entitled to the same rights as anyone else, but if they are conditionally released from prison, they must keep to the conditions. Counsellors working with clients with a history of sexual offending need sensitive and regular professional supervision.

Since the 1970s, the women's movement has focused attention on the sexual abuse of children, and 'individual women's tragedies and society's recognition of their existence has also promoted the recognition, acceptance and acknowledgement of professional counselling practice' (Perry 1993: 8). This clearly includes a greater recognition of the need for professional supervision as an integral part of the counselling process.

In Canada, where there is a national programme of group work with sexual offenders, the Correctional Service has issued guidance to staff on the limits of confidentiality. The policy makes it clear that 'The offender must fully understand the limits of confidentiality prior to the delivery of the service(s). Information will be disclosed on a "need to know basis".' It also sets out clients' rights, including that of 'informed consent' (National Committee on Sex Offender Strategy 1995: 4). This may seem punitive, but some very serious offenders remain at liberty under such group-work programmes. They have the right to refuse to join the groups, but they are likely to face prison if they do so. This raises another ethical dilemma: can effective therapy ever be delivered when there is an element of coercion by the agency? Such questions sharply highlight the differences between group work with offenders and the freer relationships normally prevailing in counselling. It is only a difference of degree, though. As case illustration 3.1 shows, such issues can and do arise in one-to-one counselling at times.

ARRANGEMENTS FOR SUPERVISION

Counselling is a specialist skill, and in many criminal justice agencies it is in short supply. One difficult consequence is that counsellors are likely to find it harder in such settings to obtain adequate professional supervision. Ways have been found to overcome this problem, but counsellors need to keep the issue on their agenda and ensure that it is not forgotten.

Case illustration 3.2

Nadia is a probation officer specializing in family court work. She spends most of her time writing court reports, but becomes involved in some longer-term work. She and her colleagues normally make explicit contracts with clients and engage in counselling with specified aims. Where resources permit, they always try to work in pairs. At present, however, she and her male colleague are 'stuck' in their work with a particular family. They have been trying to re-establish paternal contact with children whose father has been sent to prison, but the mother is using his offending as part of the argument for a 'clean break', despite a court order for regular contact.

Professional supervision is usually one to one, but they ask for a joint session with their supervisor. This takes a long time to arrange, and at the last minute the agreed appointment is cancelled by the senior officer. When they do finally see him, they try to focus the discussion on the case, but he wants to talk about their working relationship, and about further cases which he has been having difficulty in allocating. Discussing the supervision session afterwards, they are both dissatisfied.

> They cannot help feeling that the supervisor habitually evades detailed case discussions because he has little experience of counselling in the divorce-court setting.

This unsatisfactory scenario might seem an unlikely one. Unfortunately, it is all too common. Probation officers are trained as generic workers: they learn transferable skills and apply them in a variety of situations. Where they are required to specialize, additional training is provided. Management is regarded as a specialism, and middle managers are required to undergo training in it – but managers in specialist settings are not expected to prepare themselves in the same way as main-grade staff for the professional specialism itself. Thus, professional staff can find themselves supervised by people with no expertise in the specialized area of work. In such situations, some of the interventions of supervisory staff can become actively unhelpful, and peer supervision is likely to be much more productive where some aspects of professional consultation are concerned (see Brearley 1995: Chapter Four).

Strategies for dealing with this situation have varied from place to place. Some teams offer to supervise students undertaking initial training, and develop their skills in supervision by doing so. They are thus enabled to gain experience and develop expertise in staff management, and to become more involved in supervising each other's work. In these circumstances, the team manager can concentrate on defending the team's interests and holding it accountable to agency expectations and demands, without feeling that professional supervision is being neglected.

Other teams have decided to differentiate between the two kinds of supervision, and to contract with outside agencies and 'buy in' expertise on the basis of a regular consultancy, so that counselling can be professionally supervised. Elsewhere, staff have made a case for the appointment of team leaders with appropriate specialist experience who can fulfil both functions – and save the agency money in the process.

The British Association for Counselling stipulates that counsellors should receive regular supervision. The Home Office makes a similar requirement in its national standards, but these are framed in narrowly bureaucratic terms: 'The supervising officer should ensure that supervision is conducted in accordance with each National Standard and with regard to practice guidance issued by the local service concerned' (Home Office 1995: 2). While this standard can be interpreted narrowly, it need not be. The final clause offers scope for the development of more imaginative practice, of the kind described above: if local services or teams decide to give priority to professional supervision with wider aims than mere accountability through published rules, they are at liberty to do so. In an increasingly managerialist service, this may be difficult to achieve, but staff in some areas have established peer supervision arrangements that aim to improve service to clients by creating opportunities for professional discussion of individual cases between co-workers.

In voluntary agencies, the constraints are different. The probation service is cash limited and short of money; groups like Rape Crisis have no secure income and depend to a large extent upon fund raising by volunteers. Clearly, this focuses the minds of committee members when balancing different demands for expenditure. Basic services taken for granted by statutory agencies' staff, such as cleaning and secretarial work, have to be provided by volunteer counsellors in addition to their main tasks.

Another issue relating to supervision is that of staff evaluation. In statutory agencies, staff performance is assessed according to nationally prescribed criteria. Even if empathy could be measured accurately, it would be unlikely to figure among the qualities assessed for this purpose. Changes in the management culture in public services (discussed in greater detail in Chapter Five) have meant that staff are valued for more mundane abilities: how much work they can process in a given time, how often they fail to meet the targets set out in national standards, and so on. This means that, as in case illustration 3.1, priority is given to accountability issues, which are narrowly defined, when staff are supervised and their performance is assessed. As Brown (1984) has pointed out, supervision moves from bureaucratic accountability to the professional level only when it encompasses both accountability, and staff development, along with professional consultation.

A more client-centred service would assess staff very differently, and users' views would be canvassed. This was quite common in some public services in the 1980s, but it is unlikely to be accepted as part of current staff evaluation procedures in statutory agencies. Voluntary agencies have more freedom of action in this area and, where resources permit, some have developed systems for routinely obtaining feedback from clients about their services.

Workers have to *learn* to use professional supervision. In this respect, the traditional approach to staff training in the probation and social services has considerable strengths. Gardiner (1989: 81) gives the example of a trainee who was gently encouraged to see the distinction between supervision as 'a management exercise' and its potential as a two-way communication. During professional placements, such students moved 'from trying out professional, technical-type skills, and realizing that they didn't have to contain their feelings, their experience all the time, but could make use of it.'

The management of staff, and the maintenance of quality services, is clearly an important component of supervision. It should not be allowed to take over, however. This 'normative' element of supervision should be complemented by 'restorative' and 'formative' elements (Hawkins and Shohet 1990: 42; see also Tyndall 1993). Staff need line management supervision of course – but they also need support and affirmation, and supervision should contain an element of training, or at the least a process of identifying training needs.

Gardiner's book, through the use of case examples, documents this process and the accompanying shift from supervision to consultation, whereby learning becomes a more profound process of self-realization that uses the supervisory relationship as a starting point. As Gardiner points out, the bodies that validate professional social work training are in danger of stifling this process by making unduly detailed requirements that encourage surface compliance rather than real change (see also Howe 1994). Ultimately, the trend towards such over-regulation is a threat to the very therapeutic nature of the counselling professions: 'any training scheme which does not stress the importance of "therapeutic understanding" as well as skills development, will in the long run be unsuccessful' (Dryden 1991: 4). These issues are discussed further in Chapter Six.

CULTURALLY SENSITIVE SERVICE PROVISION

Counselling has developed in the context of the dominant, white culture in prosperous Western societies. It has been enriched by a wide variety of psychological traditions, but only in the past decade have questions of cultural differences and their implications for counselling practice been given due credence.

Similarly, the criminal justice system has been slow to recognize the rights and needs of black or other minority communities. The over-representation of black people in the prison system, and their under-representation among the staff of prisons and other agencies, continues (Dominelli *et al.* 1995). Counselling has an important part to play in redressing such injustice, but there is some way to go before it will be able to fulfil this function effectively. This issue will be discussed at greater length in Chapter Six.

Many of the assumptions underlying counselling are culturally biased. In itself, this is not a problem. It is clearly crucial, though, that such assumptions are made explicit, discussed and properly negotiated with people who do not share them. For example, the psychodynamic tradition leads counselling to value particular emphases more highly than other possible ways of working:

> Individuality, emphasis on past events and the detachment of the counsellor are not universal priorities; they may be of little value to counsellors and clients who do not 'belong' to the majority culture.
>
> (d'Ardenne and Mahtani 1989: ix; see also Ridley 1995)

Transcultural counselling requires a willingness to celebrate such diversity, partly by engaging with clients' experiences of struggle and their perceptions of the counselling process. Counsellors need to try to ascertain and meet needs that arise from cultural differences.

It is also important that counsellors are aware of their own underlying assumptions. Empathy can diminish with increased cultural distance between client and counsellor, and this distance needs to be actively reduced (d'Ardenne and Mahtani 1989). Research evidence suggests that for many counsellors, 'therapeutic change is judged as increased conformity to the counsellor's values' (Ridley 1995: 14; see also T. A. Kelly 1990). This has obvious implications for staff training, which are only beginning to be addressed in criminal justice settings (Dominelli *et al.* 1995). The same applies to counsellor training: 'Despite a century of research on migration and its consequences, cultural awareness in the helping professions has only begun to develop in the past twenty years' (d'Ardenne and Mahtani 1989: 9).

Indeed, counsellors may be called upon to challenge the assumptions of members of other (sometimes more prestigious) professions on behalf of their clients. The concept of culture, for example, is used in an ethnocentric way in much of psychiatric and social work practice: clients' culture is seen as problematic and thus as an explanation for their abnormal or puzzling behaviour (Fernando 1988; Ballard 1989; Denney 1992; Ridley 1995). This contributes to the over-representation of black people in custody and in secure psychiatric facilities. Counsellors, too, can inadvertently further this process because of the ways in which they assess their clients (see Ridley (1995: 61–5) on the dangers of counsellors' misuse of judgemental heuristics – routine ways of making decisions about clients, based upon practice experience – with 'minority' clients).

More positive interpretations of culturally influenced behaviour can completely change the way in which a client is assessed. The example of defendants' demeanour in court illustrates this point well. People from some ethnic groups regard it as disrespectful to make direct eye contact with people in powerful positions (Devore 1987). British courts have at times interpreted such deference by defendants as evidence of shiftiness, and sentenced them more severely. Members of other ethnic groups have developed group solidarity against oppression, and when they speak in court their use of patois is seen as evidence of disrespect and this is used against them (Ballard 1989). Thus, two more or less opposite types of behaviour are both interpreted to the disadvantage of black defendants.

Psychiatrists and psychologists also continue to use standard tests that are culturally biased (MacCarthy 1988; Ridley 1995), as do probation officers in the USA (Mann 1993). There are indications that this kind of standardized assessment instrument may become more popular in the UK. Assessments made using such tests can have enormous influence upon the subsequent treatment of clients, but it is not always easy for them or their advisors to trace the link or to challenge the use of particular tests. Counsellors and those employing counselling skills must ensure that such tests are either not used in, or at least not allowed unduly to influence, their own practice. At their best, tests are simply tools: 'They are imperfect and useful at the same time. Test results, in and of themselves, never dictate action' (Meier and Davis 1993: 67).

The dangers of a colour-blind, defensive approach, stemming from workers' desire to 'treat everyone the same', are clear. Clients who belong to oppressed groups will not enter counselling at the same point as members of the dominant group. Their self-esteem, for example, is likely to have been undermined by their experience of racism (Fernando 1986). Counsellors who are not sensitive to this 'May victimize their clients further through their lack of understanding' (Ridley 1995: 5). Sensitive counselling requires empathy with clients' experience of racist victimization that avoids the deficit model (the view that less should be expected from black people because they have suffered racism). This has to be challenged because it sets black clients up to fail and, as Ridley puts it (1995: 43), is 'unsuited for empowering minority clients'.

White counsellors' defensiveness makes it difficult for them to accept or empathize with black clients' anger. Handling such explosive issues confidently will not come easily to those not familiar with them, and the implications for training and practice are important (Lago and Thompson 1989).

A different problem, arising from unsuccessful attempts to deal with racism and its consequences, has arisen in some counselling and other agencies. Some white professionals have become 'so frightened of doing the wrong thing that they refuse to do or say anything. They attempt to escape racism by "doing nothing" but end up perpetuating the problem they seek to avoid' (Ridley 1995: 38). This process is described in some detail by recent writers on race issues affecting the work of the probation service (Denney 1992; Dominelli *et al.* 1995). It needs to be recognized and addressed, and although this has been a painful process for probation workers, it is clearly a necessary one.

Much of the difficulty seems to have arisen from inappropriate approaches to staff training, and it is important that those involved in counsellor training get to grips with this issue. Ridley's (1995) work on the racial aspects of counsellors' defensiveness is extremely helpful in this respect, and Brearley's (1995: Chapter Three) discussion of social work training and transcultural work applies equally to criminal justice settings. Counselling, like social and probation work, has something of a middle-class image, and counsellors need to be proactive in reaching out to all the groups that might make use of their services. This is discussed further in Chapter Six.

Many black clients expect and prefer a more directive style of counselling than the one to which the majority of white counsellors are accustomed (d'Ardenne and Mahtani 1989). As a counsellor,

> You need some awareness of culture as a variable in counselling, just to get an idea of how ignorant you are. You can then discuss with your clients what is of significance about their culture.
>
> (d'Ardenne and Mahtani 1989: 32)

There are specific skills involved in counselling clients whose first language is different from that of the counsellor. In some cases, an interpreter will need to be used, and it is important that counsellors know how and when to do so (Baker *et al.* 1991).

Culturally sensitive service provision cannot be prescribed by a formula: agencies have to develop appropriate policies and work out ways of implementing them. Like individual clients, the agencies within the criminal justice system begin this process from very different starting points. All have much to learn. Of the statutory agencies, the probation service is probably the most advanced, although it continues to learn from its mistakes. Its progress is documented in a number of recent books, which may provide some useful ideas for those attempting to improve practice in other parts of the system (see for example Denney 1992; Dominelli *et al.* 1995; Worrall 1995). D'Ardenne and Mahtani's (1989) and Ridley's (1995) books are extremely useful general works on race and counselling.

GENDER-SENSITIVE SERVICE PROVISION

Women comprise a minority of all types of offenders, and statutory services have tended to neglect their needs, at least until fairly recently. Counselling is now provided for women as victims of crime, but voluntary organizations have had to take the initiative in making it available, and service provision remains patchy.

The fact that the great majority of recorded crime is committed by males has been taken for granted, even by criminologists, who have tended to pathologize female offenders. Somehow, their minority status has for centuries marked women offenders out as anomalous, and their under-representation in the crime statistics has worked against them (Heidensohn 1994). Since the 1970s, the gender issues pertinent to crime have been defined and researched (Smith 1989; Perry 1993; Heidensohn 1994). Considerably more knowledge about these is now available to counsellors and others involved in the criminal justice system.

Feminist practitioners have also raised questions about the relevance of traditional psychological thought to women, arguing that:

> The theories on which many counselling models are based project both masculine and western cultural images. Developmental theorists, such as Freud and Erikson, build upon the development of male children. Experiences of male childhood and adulthood are taken as the norm. Female development is different.
>
> (Perry 1993: 41; see also Chaplin 1988; E. McLeod 1994)

Gender is also an important factor in the relationship between individual counsellors and their clients. Groups dealing with gender issues may need to be co-led by male and female workers, or single-sex groups may require facilitators of the same sex. Civil court work in the probation service is normally co-worked by two staff, one male and one female, although practice varies according to the theoretical orientation of the staff and the resources available (see James and Hay 1993). Female clients in particular feel safer with this model of co-working (Fenby 1992). In some circumstances, women who have experienced male violence or aggression may benefit from working individually or in groups with male counsellors who model positive male attitudes and behaviour (Resick and Schnicke 1993), but this is a controversial issue. Feminist counselling organizations generally prefer to rely upon women staff, both because clients are more easily able to trust them and because women workers themselves provide positive models to women clients. This is not based upon a belief that all women counsellors necessarily take a non-sexist approach, but upon experience of clients' preferences (E. McLeod 1994). There is evidence that male workers are less alert to rape trauma as a cause of clients' problems, and are more likely to be perceived as patronizing and unsupportive (Calhoun and Atkeson 1991; Barnett *et al.* 1992).

Paradoxically, women staff are in a majority in some criminal justice agencies – for example, Victim Support, Rape Crisis and the probation service – although they mainly work in the more junior positions in statutory agencies. This raises predictable difficulties when the values of managerialism clash with the caring, nurturing and client-centred approach preferred by main-grade staff, both male and female (Humphrey *et al.* 1993; Merchant 1993; Newman 1994; see also Chapters Two and Six).

Male and female counsellors need to be aware of these issues and able to put their understanding into practice. In the probation service, for example, there is a need for specific services for women clients in some particular areas. These have been successfully developed when staff have been given access to the necessary resources. Women ordered by courts to attend probation centres have often been disadvantaged by being placed in predominantly male groups, where some of their concerns are marginalized and full participation is difficult for them.

The Sheffield Probation Centre provides a good example of imaginative provision responding to women's needs. Staff there have devised a separate programme for women and they have also integrated gender issues into the curriculum of the groups for men. Instead of risking collusion with many male offenders' antisocial attitudes towards women, this provides opportunities for the men to question and explore their often unreflecting sexism. Where this is relevant to their offending, it is clearly a legitimate concern of the probation service, both in such group work and in the individual supervision that supports the programme. The women's groups meet at times convenient for clients with child-care responsibilities (for example they do not meet during school holidays) and they are staffed by women. They command the confidence of the local courts, and the Centre no longer has to return women to court in large numbers for failing to comply with gender-blind rules. Such provision requires an initial investment in terms of development time, and a degree of insight and flexibility in designing services around women's expressed needs. Not all women are involved in caring for school-age children, of course: this provision arose from research by the staff into the potential and existing client groups.

The ways in which women are assessed in criminal justice settings have been reappraised over the last 20 years (Allen 1987; Burns 1992). The process of discrimination is not always blatant, and work continues to expose and counteract more subtle forms of stereotyping. In some ways, the time has perhaps passed for further analysis of female offenders and offending. What is needed now is increased awareness that crime is predominantly a male-perpetrated problem:

> There has been a significant shift in the study of crime because of feminist perspectives on it. New ideas have been developed. The most important contribution of all, however, was to see the centrality of gender to crime and to press for that. We know a vast amount about women and crime viewed through the prism of gender. Far less is known about men and crime.
> (Heidensohn 1994: 1030–1)

Some work has now begun on masculinity and crime, including some relating specifically to counselling in criminal justice settings. To give only a few examples, Newburn and Stanko (1994) have begun to examine issues relating to men as victims of serious crime and the implications for practice. In the USA, Bridgewater (1992) has researched ways of helping male survivors of anti-gay violence. Aston (1987) has written thought provokingly about the issues involved in counselling men in prison (for both male and female staff), and Sim (1994) has provided material for a similar analysis in the British context. Burnham *et al.* (1990) have begun to set out a programme of practical action for probation officers wishing to incorporate gender awareness into their individual work with male offenders in the community. More such thinking is needed.

Counsellors working in prisons have been confronted with important ethical problems when trying to provide appropriate services to men who are HIV positive. HIV and AIDS raise a variety of difficult issues for prison staff, who need appropriate training and preparation. There have been serious problems in ensuring that prisoners have proper access to counselling, but these are gradually being overcome (Miller and Curran 1994; Bright 1995; Padel 1995). This has largely been achieved by entrusting more of the work to independent, community-based groups such as the Terrence Higgins

Trust and Scottish AIDS Monitor (Williams 1995b). In the process, important questions have been raised about prisoners' rights to counselling, to confidentiality and to medical treatment (Young and McHale 1992). The prison service has also been forced to begin to consider ways of allowing inmates a peaceful and dignified death, something taken for granted in other settings, and dealing compassionately with survivors, which is still a problem in the community as well as in prisons (Ussher 1990).

Men as perpetrators of violence against women are also beginning to receive more attention from treatment agencies. There are, inevitably, conflicts about whether resources that could be made available to help survivors of male aggression should be used to help perpetrators. Those involved in such work respond that victims can only benefit from changes to offenders' attitudes and behaviour. Group work in North America has included work on raising offenders' self-esteem (Kriner and Waldron 1988), cognitive programmes aimed at changing their attitudes to women (Eisikovits and Edleson 1989; Pence and Paymar 1993; Cyr 1994), and court-ordered projects coordinated with victim services, holding offenders to account for their behaviour (Ganley 1991; Dobash *et al.* 1995). Individual and group work with male abusers has a comparatively short history in the UK, and the few existing schemes here are experimental and temporary, and their funding is insecure (Fagg 1994). They have largely evolved from the North American examples already mentioned. Some of these projects have been thoroughly researched, and the indications are that cognitive–behavioural group-work programmes are having some success in Scotland (Dobash *et al.* 1995).

Gender awareness involves questioning stereotyped male behaviour as well as attitudes to women. Clients referred for counselling in a prison chaplaincy, for example, might initially want help with a current crisis. The focus would shift, in many such cases, to consideration of their coping skills and previous patterns of behaviour, and longer-term counselling would be negotiated. Some men would subsequently be invited to consider joining a self-help men's support group. Within such a group, they might work on issues concerning their relationships with their fathers and as fathers: 'groups can help members to work through and in some ways heal hurts sustained in earlier life' (Ratigan 1989: 91).

A few clients would progress after a time to co-counselling, and some might apply to join the prison's 'Listeners' scheme and befriend others who are suicidal (see Chapter Five). In the long term, gender-focused counselling perhaps has the potential to question and influence the macho, distorted subculture of men's prisons (Tarleton 1995), moving such issues beyond the confines of Grendon Underwood, which at the time of writing remains England's only psychiatric prison (although the Woolf Report (Woolf and Tumin 1991) proposed the establishment of several others, and this has been accepted in principle by the prison service). Counselling that raises gender issues certainly has an important role in changing thinking about and practice within the criminal justice system.

Some of the specific issues for counsellors working in criminal justice settings which have been raised above will be discussed in greater detail, with additional case illustrations, in Chapter Four.

· FOUR ·

Specific issues in counselling in criminal justice

In this chapter, some issues touched upon elsewhere in the book are considered in greater depth. Initially, the emphasis is on problems and conflicts. By way of balance, towards the end of the chapter I consider the satisfactions of working in criminal justice settings and the evidence of positive outcomes.

STRESS AND BURN-OUT

In different ways, all the work settings described in this book are stressful for counsellors. Sometimes, stress arises from the setting itself: one would expect those working with people who have been raped, people who are dying or people who have been involved in natural disasters to find this distressing, whether they work as police officers, Rape Crisis or AIDS counsellors, firefighters or psychologists. Threats to one's own life while at work can shatter previous assumptions and raise deep and frightening questions (Yarmey 1988). For other staff, less dramatic environmental hardships have a cumulative effect. For example, probation officers have described a growth in less severe, but nonetheless frightening, threats and violence against them. This can lead, over time, to a loss of confidence, difficulty in trusting clients, and ultimately, if conditions are bad enough, to burn-out (Clare 1992).

The way agencies are run, and conflicts between different organizations within a complex system like criminal justice, create other pressures that impinge upon those working in them. In some agencies, a constant sense of pressure creates a different kind of stress: staff feel as though there is a perpetual crisis, and this takes its toll on their ability to cope (Cooper and Cartwright 1994). Confusion caused by sudden changes in policy can lead to staff stress, and this is increasingly common in the public sector (Woodhouse and Pengelly 1991; Halton 1995). Stress manifests itself in a variety of ways. The specific issues it raises for counsellors in criminal justice settings include how to prevent or deal with post-traumatic stress and burn-out.

In many agencies, it is necessary to consider whether the likelihood of counsellors themselves suffering from stress is a matter that can be openly discussed. In some parts of the criminal justice system, the subculture makes it very difficult to raise such matters, although this is gradually changing (see Chapter Two). If staff feel that their careers may suffer when they ask for help with stress or burn-out, they will keep quiet and their problems may well worsen (McKenzie 1987; Duckworth 1988). Because the symptoms of post-traumatic stress disorder often coincide with depression or substance abuse (Scott and Stradling 1992), and because staff are likely to feel guilty about the things going wrong in their working lives that lead to depression or drinking problems, even serious stress is sometimes deliberately concealed. This is particularly true in working environments where professional supervision is inadequate. Counsellors need to ensure that the necessary structures are in place to prevent such situations from arising, not only for their own protection but also in the interests of their clients.

Agencies need to be made aware that stressed staff present a risk not only to themselves, but to the organization and its clientele: to give only one example, 'stressed counselors may be too inclined to take risks and push their clients' (Meier and Davis 1993: 9). The dangers to the wider community of this kind of misjudged application of pressure upon clients are obvious in criminal justice settings, where the client group includes many people with a history of violence and some with serious mental health problems.

Caring professionals and volunteers suffering from post-traumatic stress display the same symptoms as anyone else suffering similarly, but may be less inclined to seek help because of the fears mentioned above. They experience intrusive thoughts or images, they are subject to disordered arousal, and they display avoidance behaviour (Scott and Stradling 1992).

Case illustration 4.1

Malcolm is allocated the case of Mick, who is soon to be released from prison for an offence of arson. Mick has a record that includes the attempted murder of a policeman. When

Malcolm visits Mick in prison, it is clear that he resents the requirement to report to the probation office on release. He fails to keep the appointment, and Malcolm visits him at home. Mick reluctantly invites him in, and becomes very angry when Malcolm mentions that he has to report any missed appointments to the authorities. He tells Malcolm to get out of the house, and says he will kill him if he ever comes again. He adds that he knows where Malcolm lives.

Malcolm is careful in future to offer Mick appointments only in the office, and he discusses with colleagues his anxiety about supervising him. One afternoon at the end of his period of supervision, Mick comes to the office very drunk and again threatens Malcolm. He leaves, and subsequently misses his final appointment.

Rather than risk further aggression, Malcolm lets the matter go. Mick is then charged with a further assault, and when Malcolm hears that he will have to prepare a court report, he becomes very anxious. He avoids making the necessary appointment to visit Mick, and finds himself replaying his interviews with Mick repeatedly in his head, blaming himself for mishandling them. Over the next few days, he has flashbacks of the incidents when Mick threatened him. Colleagues notice that he is jumpy and irritable.

Mick breaks his bail and disappears. Malcolm is initially relieved, but his memories of the frightening incidents with Mick become increasingly intrusive. He begins to find it difficult to concentrate at work, and hard to make important decisions. He remains easily startled, and overly cautious in his dealings with clients. At staff meetings, he stops offering to take on work with clients with violent records. At home, he is irritable and secretive, and although his partner frequently asks what is wrong, he says nothing.

One day he gets drunk at lunchtime and tells a colleague what is on his mind. She suggests that he rings the confidential staff helpline, and when he does so the next day, the counsellor offers to meet him. He describes what has been happening and she offers him cognitive–behavioural counselling, telling him she thinks that he is showing signs of post-traumatic stress disorder.

Those in helping professions are not always so willing to recognize that they themselves need help. The availability of a confidential telephone counselling service (such as the one provided by local branches of the British Association of Social Workers) makes it easier for them to seek help. Non-judgemental concern shown by colleagues is important as a catalyst. Malcolm's stress was beginning to endanger his safety and his judgement, but he might not have responded well to a bald statement to that effect.

Trauma reactions are not necessarily precipitated by counsellors' direct experiences. Workers who regularly hear about the traumatic incidents in which their clients are involved sometimes find themselves suffering secondary traumatization. This usually involves counsellors experiencing intrusive recollections or nightmares in which clients' accounts feature. One's own relationships can be disrupted, and the extent to which one feels safe at home and going about one's ordinary business can also be affected. This kind of reaction can interfere with the counselling process, because traumatic reactions often include avoidance, and counsellors may try (not always consciously) to prevent clients from talking about similar incidents. For this reason and for their own welfare, people suffering secondary trauma should seek help (Resick and Schnicke 1993).

Post-traumatic stress disorder is at one end of a continuum. A certain degree of stress is healthy, but agencies should monitor staff stress. The most obvious method is through individual supervision, but this is not always sufficient, as discussed in Chapter Three. Other possibilities include the provision of occupational health and confidential staff counselling schemes, stress audits, courses on stress management, staff 'awaydays' and career break schemes.

Organizations also need to develop ways of monitoring stress in order to avoid, or at least to detect, staff burn-out. When the pressures of work place inordinate demands upon staff, some eventually develop dysfunctional coping mechanisms: bureaucratic strategies for limiting the workload; bad temper; emotional distance from – and depersonalization of – clients, and so on. Burn-out results in frustration, cynicism, loss of motivation, the inappropriate expression of 'gallows' humour, and feelings of being cornered and having no choices (Burnard 1991), as well as the physical symptoms of stress-related illnesses. Often, such staff will return to their duties with renewed enthusiasm after quite a short break; simple flexibility about arrangements for time off can make a big difference in stressful occupations. Research has also shown that management structures that facilitate considerate treatment of staff can prevent whole staff groups from burning out simultaneously (Vachon 1987).

Organizations need to find ways of showing staff and volunteers that they are appreciated and cared for. Consultation and case discussions between staff should be encouraged and valued, not least because they provide opportunities to ventilate stress. In particular, staff supervision should involve regular reviews of workloads and discussion of the rewards available to staff – including study time, courses and opportunities for professional development. Supervisory staff also need to be prepared to tackle the structural causes of staff stress and burn-out. This will not always be easy: structural causes might include such intractable problems as shortage of staff and resources, ideological conflicts between funders and service providers, and bureaucratic methods of service organization. Nevertheless, it is surely better to acknowledge and where appropriate confront such stressors than to appear to blame individual staff for their stress (Handy 1990).

ASSESSMENT AND BIAS

The dangers of cultural and gender bias when using standardized tests and assessment methods have been discussed in Chapter Three. There is a more general, and more insidious, danger for counsellors in criminal justice and related agencies. Clients may have been assessed by others before being referred for counselling. In the process, some filtering of referrals may have occurred. This can operate in a number of ways that are disadvantageous to potential clients from oppressed groups, and the referral process needs to be scrutinized with this in mind.

Project illustration 4.1
A Victim Support scheme in a multiracial area had always recruited volunteers through the local volunteer bureau. This system had operated for a number of years without any noticeable problems arising. Victim Support in the area began to pay increasing attention to assisting clients who were victims of racially motivated crime, and scheme staff found that most such clients preferred to be seen by volunteers of the same race.

The scheme's coordinator realized that they had only one black volunteer, who began to find that she was unable to cope with all the referrals being made to her, particularly as several of her cases required long-term help. The scheme asked the volunteer bureau for the names of more black volunteers, and it was unable to suggest any. The coordinator raised the matter with the scheme's committee. It was decided that she should seek invitations to give talks to local groups to which potential black volunteers belonged, and also to advertise in two local free papers specifically for volunteers from particular racial groups.

When funding became available for a second staff member, it was agreed that consideration would be given to appointing a specialist racial harassment worker (see Kimber and Cooper (1991) for details of a number of such appointments).

In this example, it is volunteers rather than clients who have been inadvertently filtered. The effect of the filtering process is that an equal service is not available to potential black and white clients. In the case example, a proactive decision was taken to improve the scheme's services to black communities, which had not until then been well served in relation to racial harassment, an area of great concern to them. Only then did the scheme realize that it had accepted without question the fact that its volunteer workforce was unrepresentative of the local community in an important respect.

In the agency used in this example, referrals of *client*s are not necessarily filtered. Victim Support schemes have a range of different types of agreement with their local police about which victims of crime are referred to them. Some scheme coordinators look at the papers relating to every crime in their area that has a personal victim, and decide how to respond. Other schemes agree criteria with the police, who then filter referrals. In some areas, victims of racially motivated offences are a priority, as in the example above.

Once a filtering process is established by any agency or service, it is susceptible to bias, as with all human judgements. The police tend not to view inter-racial incidents as racially motivated, even when a black victim tells them otherwise. This not unnaturally leads to a perception that crime motivated by racial hatred is taken less seriously than other types of offence (House of Commons Home Affairs Committee 1989; Senior 1993a; Smith 1995). If other agencies work with black clients who are racially harassed or attacked, or discuss offences with clients, they must take the possibility of racial motivation seriously. Failing to do so repeats the mistakes often made by the police, and effectively subjects clients to repeat victimization by the agency (Senior 1993a).

Where issues about the relevance of service to black communities arise, an agency such as Victim Support has to work harder than usual to maintain its openness to groups in need of support and counselling. If it does not undertake outreach work of the kind described in case illustration 4.1, it is in danger of being perceived as part of the problem of racism rather than as part of the solution to it.

Many of the same issues apply to the selection of students for training as probation officers, social workers, clinical psychologists and so on. Unless training programmes are aware of the need for antidiscriminatory recruitment procedures, they are not likely to find that the students eventually selected are fully representative of society. Outreach work is likely to be needed here also (see Brearley 1995: Chapter Four). Agency and college staff need to build up their own awareness of the ways in which discrimination works, both directly and indirectly, and find ways of ensuring that they do not themselves become part of the problem. Similar arguments apply to the issue of client access to services, as case illustration 4.2 shows.

Case illustration 4.2

Winston is an unemployed black man aged 25. He is appearing in court for failing to pay a fine, imposed six months earlier for not having a television licence. The magistrates have to determine whether he has wilfully refused to pay, or whether there are extenuating circumstances. He is not represented by a solicitor, and he says very little when the clerk of the court asks him questions. He is asked why he has not made at least some attempt to pay, and he says he does not know.

The magistrates adjourn briefly to discuss the case. The duty probation officer takes the opportunity to suggest to Winston that he obtains legal representation. When the magistrates return, Winston asks if he can have a solicitor, and the case is adjourned. The probation officer stands up and suggests that a means enquiry report might be of assistance to the court. The magistrates have the power to request such a report, but had not thought of doing so. They readily agree.

The probation officer discusses the matter in her next supervision session, and her senior officer agrees to place it on the agenda of the Probation Liaison Committee (a regular forum in which probation staff meet magistrates). The clerk and the magistrates present at the meeting are defensive about any suggestion that people are imprisoned unnecessarily in their courts, or that black people fare any worse than whites. The Committee agrees to receive statistics at its next meeting on the extent to which imprisonment is used for fine default, and the senior probation officer offers to apply for funding in order to provide a fuller duty officer service for the fines court if the statistics suggest that this is needed.

There was a real danger that Winston would have been sent to prison, without the probation service having any opportunity to become involved. (In fact, in many areas, staff resourcing difficulties mean that it is not possible to provide a duty probation officer regularly for fines courts.) Because he has been referred to the probation service, he will at least have the opportunity to give an account of his circumstances to someone with the counselling skills to listen sympathetically and make an informed assessment. It might be argued that the failure of the magistrates to refer him earlier, and the failure of the clerk to advise him to get a solicitor, were examples of institutional racism. It is in the nature of such arguments that they are difficult to prove. Many white people also go to prison for non-payment of fines imposed for trivial offences. What the case clearly does show is that staff have to be prepared to intervene in the chain of referral if they are to avoid injustice.

So far, this discussion has concentrated upon issues of access to services. Counsellors also need to consider issues of accessibility: are some styles of counselling more applicable to particular client groups? Evidence is becoming available that suggests that some approaches to counselling are culture specific, and this clearly merits further research. Kohlberg's theories about moral development, for example, underpin much of cognitive–behavioural counselling, but his notion of higher stages of moral development is culturally biased and gender biased. It appears to apply to complex urban societies and middle-class populations, but not to fit so well when attempts are made to use it in assessing people from 'traditional folk cultures or in working-class communities', which give higher priority to virtues other than those emphasized by Kohlberg (Snarey 1985: 226). This presents real problems for counsellors in Australia, Canada, New Zealand and the United States who are working with aboriginal clients using this theoretical model. It may also have implications for counselling members of other ethnic minorities, and for work in rural areas and with working-class clients. Once again, the theory also has more relevance to men than to women.

In Canada, some of the problems of the criminal justice system in dealing with a diverse and geographically dispersed population are being addressed in imaginative ways. Increasingly, court disposals such as community service orders and restitution programmes (whereby offenders directly compensate victims of crime) are being devolved to local communities. Councils of tribal elders and voluntary organizations are taking these schemes over (Griffiths and Patenaude 1992; Bracken 1995). Both in the community and inside prisons, aboriginal healing lodges are working towards the rehabilitation of offenders. In the cities, there are proposals for analogous provisions, such as the Native Probation Unit in Manitoba (Harper and Charter 1993). At government level, there is a growing recognition that (as the Commissioner of the Correctional Service of Canada put it at a conference in 1995):

> if we look at the thousands of years during which northern aboriginal peoples existed in harmony with nature and as peoples, it is presumptuous for us to think that you cannot design corrections in a way to better serve your social needs.
>
> (Edwards 1995: 9)

While direct comparisons are not possible, there may be useful lessons which can be learned from these initiatives with respect to the relationship between the criminal justice system and black people in other countries, including the United Kingdom. One important lesson, however, is that experiments such as the healing lodges can rebound upon black offenders. While it is true that in Canada the federal prison for women has been closed, and replaced for aboriginal women by the healing lodges, the number of federal prison places has simultaneously been considerably expanded (from 120 beds, about two-thirds of which are occupied by aboriginal women, to about 380). The healing lodges are secure institutions, albeit closer to home for many of the prisoners, and demonstrate the limitations and contradictions of trying to incorporate woman-centred therapeutic ideals in a prison environment (I am grateful to Dr Karlene Faith of Simon Fraser University, Vancouver, for this information; see also Hannah-Moffat 1995).

One of the valuable insights of the Canadian experiments is that it is possible to recognize the links between child abuse and offending not only theoretically, but also in practice. Perhaps for the first time, groups such as the Ontario Native Women's Association, the Native Clan Organization in Winnipeg and the Indigenous Women's Collective of Manitoba have proposed the creation of facilities with holistic approaches to crime and abuse. In some circumstances, they argue for counselling in the same healing lodges for abusers and other types of offenders, victims and family members. On the other hand, some have advocated placing the treatment of aboriginal male sex offending under women's control.

Under Maori justice in New Zealand, abusers are exiled and counselled by tribal elders, who decide when they should be allowed to return (Consedine 1995). These approaches would pose all kinds of problems within the existing framework of conventional social services, but the progress of these experiments will be interesting to observe.

The Native Clan Organization runs separate groups for aboriginal sexual offenders, in the belief that their experiences of racism, displacement and disadvantage necessitate culturally relevant correctional programmes. The teachings of tribal elders recognize alcohol misuse, family violence and offending as symptomatic of a fundamental disharmony, not merely the acts of evil individuals. As such, this approach also incorporates holistic approaches. Having reviewed their earlier programmes, which were available to all sections of the community, the Organization found that the outcomes were less favourable for aboriginal offenders (as they are in many community correctional programmes run by the state corrections services). They then experimented with incorporating traditional ceremonial healing in the programme for aboriginal offenders, as well as using the latest knowledge about what works with sex offenders generally. In some of the new treatment groups, cognitive–behavioural counselling and ceremonies thousands of years old are being brought together (Native Clan Organization 1995).

The political significance of these experiments is enormous. For once:

> The very authority that disempowered traditional Aboriginal means of keeping order by displacing the Aboriginal peacemaking is now being applied to restore respect for Aboriginal justice measures.
>
> (Mandamin 1993: 289)

Similar arguments are being made in New Zealand and Australia, where experiments in reinstating traditional, restorative systems of justice are having some success (Braithwaite and Daly 1994; Consedine 1995), although there is some evidence that more needs to be done to empower victims of crime to take a full part in the discussions (Morris *et al.* 1993). Such insights are not directly transferable to the UK situation, where the traditions and the patterns of migration are very different, but we may be able to learn from the North American and Australasian experiences. Like aboriginal peoples, some minority groups in the UK have rich traditions relating to the resolution of disputes, and are interested in exercising a degree of self-determination.

At present, our criminal justice system and most staff working individually with offenders take little interest in their cultural and religious backgrounds. Initial assessment of clients should perhaps take account of such traditions, and counsellors, like other caring professionals, should improve their levels of cultural awareness.

Where there is scope for extending the use of restorative rather than punitive approaches to offending, this should be explored. The British and American criminal justice systems have pursued retributive approaches almost to their logical endpoint, with terrifying results in terms of incarceration and reoffending rates, and in terms of suicide and self-harm. An enormous proportion of our young men have had prison experience, and there is no sign that this is discouraging crime: on the contrary, criminalized young people reoffend at an alarming rate. Restorative justice of the kind described in a number of case studies (Maxwell and Morris 1993; Consedine 1995) offers real hope that there may be positive alternatives to retributive thinking.

As with race issues, so gender dimensions of clients' problems are frequently overlooked in the criminal justice system. Although a very high proportion of women offenders have a background of being sexually abused as children, the relevance of this aspect of their experience is often not properly taken into account when female clients are assessed. Even when probation officers do mention a history of sexual abuse in pre-sentence reports for courts, its relevance to the offences under consideration is not always made clear.

Case illustration 4.3

Ellen is serving a prison sentence for a series of offences of fraud committed while she was using heroin. With the support of her outside probation officer, she has moved to a prison with a drug-free wing. Although there are still opportunities to misuse drugs, she has avoided these.

Thinking about her past, she feels that many of her problems stem from being sexually abused by her stepfather when she was 14. She left home soon afterwards, and has been homeless for much of the last two years. She mentions to the probation officer when he visits that she has been depressed and anxious, having nightmares and washing compulsively. He seems to think that this may be a result of her withdrawal from heroin.

By chance, another prisoner, Morag, notices her washing her hands for the fifth time early one morning. She tells her about the two counsellors from the nearby city who visit the prison every week, and offers to take her to meet one of them.

Ellen attends a group meeting with Morag the following week. She discovers that the counsellors are from a Rape Crisis centre, and that they offer individual counselling to prisoners who have experienced sexual abuse. After attending the group for another couple of weeks, she asks to see one of the counsellors. They soon begin to work on issues relating to her abuse, her reaction to stress and her feelings about men. She decides to continue seeing the counsellor at the Rape Crisis centre after her release.

As McLeod notes (1994: 122), women clients of a feminist therapy centre repeatedly spoke warmly of 'how the unusual experience of not having their feelings and efforts defined as inferior began to make them feel better'. She interviewed Winifred, who said of her counsellor that 'What helped me tremendously is her saying, "There is a reason for this and it's not your fault".'

In case illustration 4.3, Ellen's needs were not fully met by her male probation officer. Luckily, she was in a prison with an unusual level of provision for women in her situation (see Marchant (1993) for a description of Manchester Rape Crisis centre's service for women at Styal Prison). By chance, a fellow prisoner thought to suggest that she contact the counsellors. Many abused women do go to prison for apparently unrelated offences (Carlen *et al.* 1985; Padel and Stevenson 1988). Service provision that addresses the needs of abused women is in its infancy, and there is limited awareness within the prison system of the need for such services. Projects such as the one at Styal are important because they provide a counselling service to a stigmatized group where it is needed, and because they do so in a non-directive way that makes it clear that 'There is a reason for this and it's not your fault' (see 'T' 1988). They are necessary, but wherever possible earlier intervention is needed in order to prevent the inappropriate imprisonment of women in the first place (Hannah-Moffat 1995).

ROLE CONFLICTS FOR COUNSELLORS IN CRIMINAL JUSTICE SETTINGS

Social workers and probation officers have always had to balance the need to offer care with the requirement to undertake control. This oversimplified contrast, 'care versus control', has been the subject of endless controversy within the profession. It is an important debate, because it raises profound questions about the purpose and ethics of social work intervention. Counsellors in criminal justice settings need to be aware of these discussions, because they have implications for their work.

In Chapter Three, some of the dynamics of care and control in the probation and prison systems were reviewed. This chapter concentrates upon conflicts between the disciplinary or controlling role and the counselling role. Chapter Five goes on to look at professional boundaries and inter-agency relations.

One of the difficulties that has arisen from careless use of the term counselling is particularly acute in criminal justice settings. As Woolfe *et al.* (1989) have pointed out, there is a tendency for non-specialists to use the word counselling to endow any advisory or even persuasive activity (from 'debt counselling' to 'double glazing counselling') with an innocent and reassuring sound. The suspicion many clients in criminal justice settings feel about counselling is partly explained by this trend. In the USA, for example, a textbook on counselling in criminal justice settings refers to electric shock treatment as a counselling technique, and goes on to argue that 'the American system of criminal justice . . . gives orders and tells offenders what they must do. Directive counseling modalities allow the criminal justice counselor to do the same' (Masters 1994: 113)! Masters does later put the arguments against such an approach, but she is not alone in arguing that authoritarian approaches may form a legitimate part of the repertoire of counsellors.

Another American writer claims that the roles of counsellor and of law enforcement officer conducting an interrogation of a client suspected of reoffending 'do not necessarily conflict' (Walsh 1992: 50). In a revealing discussion, he advises that clients should be 'read their rights' before such interviews, and that this kind of discussion need not always compromise the potential for productive counselling in future. It is difficult to see how a counsellor can interrogate a client about criminal offences in one interview and expect to return to a counselling relationship in the next: there is clearly a different view of the nature of counselling from that held by the majority of counsellors in operation in some parts of the American criminal justice system.

In the UK, there is a parallel tendency (particularly in the probation service, but also among prison staff and psychologists) to speak and write about 'confronting' clients with their offending behaviour and its consequences, with rather combative connotations. This may well be a valuable activity, but not as a part of counselling. The notion of confrontation in this sense raises ethical and practical questions. Counselling depends upon a trusting relationship, which is likely to be jeopardized by the aggressive style of discussion sometimes involved in confronting clients about their behaviour. Counselling proceeds from a contract, and it is hard to imagine a genuine consultation between a counsellor and a client which led to confrontation being agreed as an objective. It is also difficult to envisage potentially constructive outcomes of such a contract if it did.

Clients' offending or offensive behaviour can be the focus of discussion without any need for confrontation. The term has been widely misunderstood in work with offenders, and perhaps to some extent it has also been misappropriated for political reasons. In a climate where politicians demand that probation and prison services should 'get tough', and are prepared to intimidate and bully opponents (Faulkner 1995), there is a temptation to placate the powerful by using macho, pugnacious language when discussing the services' work with offenders. The danger of this is that agencies lose sight of their values in their anxiety to appease people who have no sympathy with such values. The probation service in England and Wales, for example, was offered the opportunity by the Home Office in the late 1980s to move to 'centre stage' in the criminal justice system. In exchange, it was expected to treat offenders more punitively: many would say more harshly and less compassionately. The danger is that 'you sell out on your values to get in there at the centre' (Tarleton 1995), although some senior staff have been able to assert the importance of humanistic values in their dealings with the Home Office (Rutherford 1993).

Some practitioners, however, have wholeheartedly embraced the idea of confronting clients. For some reason, many people who work with sexual offenders feel that this kind of offending is so repugnant that the counselling values they espouse in their other work can be suspended. This seems unlikely to be effective, if only because it ignores the possibility of working with clients' denial:

> We should be more concerned with concentrating upon the significance and function of denial than with attempting to prevent its manifestations. Once clients are aware that our acceptance of them is not incompatible with our abhorrence at their activities then their need to deny as a means of shoring up their self image becomes less necessary.
>
> (Sheath 1990: 161)

It is possible – and advisable – to be direct in discussing offending with clients, but there is no need to be aggressive. In counsellors' use of the idea of confrontation, this distinction is clearly made: 'Confrontation in counseling does not mean opposing the client but pointing out discrepancies between clients' goals and their actions' (Meier and Davis 1993: 12). This is confrontation in the sense of encouraging clients to consider the logic – or the lack of it – in their thinking and their actions. In other words, it is confronting people with inconsistencies in their accounts and behaviour. It is a far cry from rubbing people's noses aggressively in what they have done.

The consequences of the misinterpretation of this concept in criminal justice settings are serious. Psychologists and probation officers who have taken the idea of confrontation literally can do a great deal of damage, increasing clients' resentment and mistrust and missing opportunities to engage in more constructive relationships. The rhetoric of 'confronting offending behaviour' was intended to encourage staff to focus on the reasons why people became clients, and in that respect it had positive potential. Unfocused work had led to net widening, whereby clients were drawn into the criminal justice system under supervision because they were identified as having problems with which they needed help. Often, such assistance was available elsewhere, and there was no need to label these individuals as clients (Smith 1995). The idea of confronting offending was introduced in order to avoid this danger, but it holds dangers of its own.

In counselling practice, in criminal justice settings as elsewhere, the relationship between counsellor and client is what we believe leads to change. It is nourished by careful listening on the counsellor's part, and preaching has no place in it. Adherence to values such as non-judgementalism is not only possible when working with offenders, it is indispensable (Williams 1995a). Meier and Davis (1993: 12), drawing upon the work of Egan, offer a sensible piece of advice:

> A good rule of thumb is that you can confront as much as you've supported. . . . Support and empathy are the foundation upon which the counseling relationship is built. Consequently, confrontation is unwise during the early stages of counseling. However, once you have established a bond, confrontation may increase client self-awareness and motivation to change.

Some offenders feel guilt about their behaviour – not only their offending – and counselling ideally provides a safe place for this to be discussed and resolved. The design of prisons in the eighteenth and early nineteenth centuries (many of which are still in use) reflected the belief that inmates should be forced to reflect upon their misdeeds in solitude. This form of mortification was associated with religious idealism, and was not especially successful. All the same, the parole system in Western countries rests upon the same sort of assumptions: prisoners are considered ready to be released only when they have shown an appropriate degree of remorse. Prisoners' guilt remains a problem that the system has done little to address, yet so much might be achieved in terms of rehabilitation if individuals were given opportunities to work on such issues. A number of life sentence prisoners have told me over the years that their victims were in their minds every day. Some felt that this fact was of interest to the system only as a potential paragraph in a parole report, yet complex and ambiguous feelings were at stake. Offenders should perhaps be expected to display remorse, but not as part of a performance for staff who are assessing their suitability for release.

Discussing guilt about horrific offences is not easy. It depends upon a trusting relationship, and one within which offenders can be confident that they will be treated with respect.

It is not always possible in criminal justice settings to avoid a degree of confrontation, because staff do not have the luxury of prolonged involvement with certain groups of clients. When preparing a report for a criminal court, for example, some confrontation may be necessary in order to establish a client's motivation in committing an offence. Nevertheless, Meier and Davis are undoubtedly right that it is better done when client and worker know and trust each other, and this is often the basis of recommendations for community supervision. People's motives are frequently subtle and deep-rooted, and counselling can help to uncover them. This may be the only way to achieve lasting change, and it is the main rationale for the existence of the probation order (which effectively postpones the confrontation until after a working relationship has been formed), and for much of the counselling provision in prisons and the community. A gradual approach that addresses the issues sensitively, and even indirectly at first, is more likely to succeed (Sheath 1990).

The same applies to the collection of evidence by the police in cases where people have been sexually abused. The insensitivity exposed by Roger Graef's documentary film about the investigation of rape cases by Thames Valley Police in 1982 should no longer occur. Unfortunately, this does not mean that police officers interviewing survivors of abuse can escape the professional conflicts involved in counselling potential witnesses. The boundaries need to be made very explicit when a police officer is helping complainants in rape or sexual abuse cases, and appropriate referrals made for further counselling.

A form of confrontation is used by some counsellors working with rape survivors. Careful questioning can help the client 'confront her stuck points' (Resick and Schnicke 1993: 74). Raped women may find a number of obstacles to healing, including feelings of guilt about failing to prevent the incident or not fighting back hard enough against the perpetrator. Resick and Schnicke show, using case illustrations, how to counsel such clients using sympathetic but challenging questions. An alternative method is the use of trauma belief inventories (Scott and Stradling 1992), which also offer a method of challenging and helping to correct clients' cognitive biases, their beliefs about the world having been distorted by the traumatic event.

CONTRACTS, DEFENSIVENESS AND DENIAL

Counselling normally involves some form of contract between client and counsellor, although the degree of formality with which it is reached and recorded varies according to the style of counselling being employed. At the very least, counsellors pass on to clients their own understanding of what counselling is about and how it can help them. In criminal justice settings, there is considerable variation in the extent to which clients are introduced to such issues, both because many clients come reluctantly and because some staff who are unsympathetic to counselling nevertheless have a role in its provision.

Prison officers, for example, help to draw up sentence plans, which are effectively contracts between individual prisoners and the prison system. Often, they initiate the sentence planning process. If their contribution to it is perceived by the prisoner as unhelpful, this can prejudice relationships between him or her and potential counsellors, who also participate in later stages of sentence planning. Prison officers receive no training in counselling (unless they undertake it in their own time) and they are unlikely to think of explaining sentence planning to inmates in any detail. Thus, the process gets off to a bad start, and resistance to future discussion of sentence plans is highly likely.

How can any counsellor form a meaningful contract with a reluctant client? On the face of it, the question is self-contradictory. Yet counsellors in all settings frequently face clients' resistance: the difference is only one of degree. Part of the skill involved in counselling is in observing possible resistance and deciding how or whether to deal with it. Sometimes it is simply noted. On other occasions it is addressed, not necessarily head on, but deliberately. Offenders are likely to be resistant to the whole idea of counselling, not least because it is somebody else, not them, who has decided it may be of benefit to them. Where involuntary clients are involved, complex issues of competing values arise, but these are entirely susceptible to discussion with the client: indeed, such negotiation is likely to be beneficial (Hutchinson 1992). One strategy for addressing resistance to counselling itself is to delay discussing a contract until the client's feelings about entering counselling have been fully explored. It is entirely reasonable for people to resent being 'sentenced to therapy', and this perception can often be reframed more positively. Counselling can be 'portrayed as an opportunity to increase freedom by pointing out that the process is designed not to restrict but to increase alternatives' open to the client (Harris 1991).

Criminal justice clients often employ powerful defences to avoid discussion of their offending. So do criminal justice professionals, who may find discussion of some offences distasteful or frightening (Williams 1992b). People who have committed serious offences frequently find that they cannot remember much about them: this is often an example of repression or denial. Other serious offenders display different types of defences, including intellectualization and rationalization, to avoid discussion of their offending. Men who sexually assault women or children, for example, frequently believe that their victims enjoy participating in the offences. Such a major rationalization clearly has to be questioned, but this is done most effectively if it is done by the offender himself. Failing that, group work can be helpful, if it provides opportunities for other offenders to challenge the client's distorted thinking: they are likely to be 'experts at identifying their fellow sex offenders' thinking patterns' (Masters 1994: 59). Clients are likely to take notice of each other in this context rather more readily than listening to counsellors' views about their behaviour and attitudes. Group work of this kind offers powerful ways of challenging entrenched antisocial attitudes.

Case illustration 4.4

Trevor is describing his 'index' offence (the one for which he was sentenced) to the other members of a sex offenders' group at a probation centre. He has written a list of triggers, factors which for him lead up to offending, as part of his homework since the previous meeting of the group. When he reads out one of these trigger points, he is challenged by another member of the group.

Trevor: 'I'm too shy to talk to women, I don't like them to think I'm trying to pick them up.'

Jim: 'Wouldn't you rather people thought you were a womanizer, than have them know you're a child molester?'

The directness of this challenge is shocking, but it is not made in an aggressive way, because Jim is in the same position as Trevor, and they both know it. In such circumstances, denial can and will be challenged. The group setting, once a group is working well, makes this easier for staff, but they have to create the environment for this carefully. In one-to-one work, denial also has to be dealt with, but it is not always easy to do so without the client feeling attacked.

The insights gained during group work can also be built upon in individual counselling. There is a danger that in group work, offenders may simply be taught how to say the right thing, and in the process become more plausible without changing their attitude to offending. This is more difficult to sustain in the context of a strong one-to-one counselling relationship (albeit not impossible). There is, as Harris (1991) points out, an important distinction to be made between surface compliance, the mere discontinuation of the expression of irrational or antisocial thoughts and beliefs, and a deeper change of the client's personal constructs and patterns of thinking and beliefs. Considerable success has been claimed for treatment regimes at 'therapeutic' prisons such as Grendon Underwood in England, which address serious offending on both these levels simultaneously. Neither in group sessions nor in individual counselling are members of the therapeutic group allowed to avoid issues relating to their offending (see Genders and Player 1995). There is no reason to think that the custodial element of the therapy contributes to its success, however. Grendon's inmates are there because they are dangerous or because the seriousness of their offending was judged to justify incarceration. Some equally serious offenders are successfully counselled in the community (see Beckett *et al.* 1995).

Counsellors in criminal justice settings have to avoid trying to rescue clients who resist involvement in counselling. There will often be unpleasant consequences for the client of not undertaking counselling. In prisons, it may prejudice parole (or in Grendon's therapeutic communities, it often leads to prisoners being returned to conventional prisons). After release, it can lead to clients being recalled to prison. In the community, it frequently ends in clients being returned to court in breach of probation orders. Counsellors have a responsibility to point out these consequences, and to note the self-punitive aspect of failure to comply, but not to preach to clients about the need to obey court orders or conditions of release. Indeed, it can be important to acknowledge the indignity involved in being in custody, or being required to undergo counselling. In some circumstances, it may be appropriate to show one's admiration for the client's dignity in the face of humiliating penalties, and one's understanding of the coping strategies they use (Williams 1991). As Harris and Watkins (1987: 45) put it: 'clients who chafe at the involuntary nature of their positions may be showing the noblest aspiration of the human spirit: the desire to be free and self-determining'.

Counsellors can value this spirit in their clients and show positive regard for it, while also recognizing that there are inevitable limits to freedom and responsibilities that accompany the exercise of these freedoms.

In the context of alcohol counselling, Harris (1991) points out how hard it can be to watch clients doing avoidable damage to themselves. He suggests, however, that to rescue such clients continually from the unpleasant consequences of failing to take advantage of counselling is actually a form of co-dependency. Only when clients have seen these consequences for themselves, and only if they see positive benefits in committing themselves to counselling, can a workable contract be established. The same applies to work with offenders in general.

Where victims of crime are concerned, there is a further problem in relation to contracts. Victims may experience an approach from a counsellor as intrusive, but there is often no other way of offering them a real choice about whether to ask for help. This issue is not unique to the criminal justice setting, and it relates to the victims of large-scale disasters as well as those of personal crimes. Counsellors can usefully make themselves available, but they must be sure to hear and comply when potential clients ask them to go away.

Most Victim Support schemes operate a system of 'cold calling'. Their volunteers simply turn up at the door of people who have been personal victims of crime, and ask if they can help. In more than a third of the cases they are referred by the police (Maguire 1991). Regular lists of crimes with personal victims are supplied to Victim Support schemes soon after these are reported to the police, and scheme coordinators decide which cases should be allocated to volunteers. This model of working derives from a view of the community as one in which people owe each other a duty of care, as good neighbours. It does not fully take account of a number of issues, including the potential dangers to volunteers involved in unannounced visits of this kind, and the complexity of many social conflicts that are recorded as crimes. The person who, on paper, is a victim of assault may have been involved in a fight where the police had great difficulty in determining who was the aggressor and who the aggrieved party. Not surprisingly in such circumstances, the Victim Support volunteer's visit may be unwelcome. It is, however, quite rare for victims to complain about such unsolicited visits, and Maguire and Corbett (1987) found that over 80 per cent of victims receiving such visits welcomed this. A good deal depends upon the approach taken by volunteers when they first introduce themselves, and their ability to explain the reason for their visit succinctly.

With some types of offence, cold calling would seem to be particularly inappropriate: people recovering from the trauma of a sexual assault, for example, are likely to be cautious about whom they invite into their homes. Most Victim Support schemes are sensitive to this distinction, and they screen referrals before allocating them to volunteers. A few of the clients not visited 'cold' are telephoned; most receive a letter. The take-up rate is, perhaps not surprisingly, lower in these cases (Maguire 1991). Victim Support in many areas now refers sexual assault cases to Rape Crisis centres, which are much better equipped to offer the kind of long-term counselling that is likely to be needed (Kosh and Williams 1995). Most schemes do nevertheless deal with rape referrals, at least initially. This was an area of work they avoided until the mid-1980s, but it has increased rapidly. In some areas, there is a less cordial relationship between Victim Support and Rape Crisis schemes, and there are signs that the police prefer to deal with Victim Support, on whose local committees they are always represented. Such conflicts need to be overcome if clients' best interests are to be served.

The Home Office took an initiative in relation to the handling of victims of crime by criminal justice agencies when, in 1990, it issued a pamphlet called the Victim's Charter (Home Office 1990) which purported to set out the rights of victims.

Some provisions of the Victim's Charter have caused serious difficulties because insufficient thought was given to the implications of contacting victims of crime (and the survivors of murder victims). The Charter suggests that probation officers preparing reports about day release or short home leaves for lifers and other serious offenders towards the end of their sentences should contact victims or their families to ascertain their views. Many such contacts have caused serious problems for people who thought they had come to terms with the loss of a loved one, only to have the matter reopened without warning. Even some of the staff carrying out such interviews have acknowledged that it has been done insensitively (Aubrey and Hossack 1994; Kosh and Williams 1995). As one probation officer put it, reflecting upon such an interview carried out by telephone:

> You're not there to support the victim when they need it and you're not there to pick up the pieces afterwards. You need a lot of support in place before you plough in with your big feet as I did.
>
> (Kosh and Williams 1995: 31)

As a result of these early problems, local Victim Support schemes have now reached agreements with many probation services about ways of working together to support victims of serious crimes. In some places, a pragmatic decision was taken to implement the Victim's Charter provision only in respect of new offences, so that victims and their families could be given an explicit choice about whether to have any further contact with the probation service. This elementary principle of counselling had not been taken into account by the civil servants who drafted the Charter.

TRAINING NEEDS AND OPPORTUNITIES

There are many different types of opportunity for counselling to be used in criminal justice settings, as outlined in previous chapters. Such work is demanding, and requires preparation and training. This section briefly considers the provision for this, although it is only a selective account.

Volunteers are used by several agencies. The voluntary agencies also have some paid staff, but rely primarily upon volunteers. In the case of Women's Aid and Victim Support, such volunteers require little formal training. The minimum requirement is attendance at a three-day course for Victim Support volunteers, although there are opportunities for further training to work with specific client groups. The emphasis of the basic course is mainly on listening skills and preparation for advising clients about practical issues such as security, compensation claims and so on.

Most agencies also hold regular support meetings for their volunteers. Rape Crisis centres require their volunteers to complete a basic, general counselling course before joining an induction course providing training specific to the setting, which may be up to 12 days long ('T' 1988), although not all centres operate such an intensive course. In some smaller centres, volunteer training is provided by students during placements, or on a 'cascade' basis, where those few members who have received training pass on what they have learnt to others (Root and Davies 1995). Some Victim Support schemes now have specialist courses for volunteers counselling raped women (for details see Corbett and Hobdell 1988). More sophisticated and centralized training is required for marriage guidance counselling, and there is also advanced training available that qualifies counsellors to assist couples experiencing sexual dysfunction and couples seeking conciliation when they have decided to separate. Relate (formerly the National Marriage Guidance Council) invites the partners of volunteers training as sex therapists to attend part of the basic certificate course (which all volunteer counsellors undertake) with them. This recognizes the likely effect of such training upon volunteers' relationships with others (Tyndall 1993).

Some of the statutory agencies also use volunteers. The obvious example is the probation service, which takes up references and also undertakes criminal record checks before allocating work to volunteers (as do some voluntary agencies whose work brings their volunteers into contact with children or other vulnerable people). There is then a brief induction course (usually held in the evening, over several weeks) and a regular support meeting with staff. In some areas, the probation service has handed over completely or partly the organization of volunteering to the Society of Voluntary Associates (SOVA). This has a similar system of recruiting, training and supporting volunteers to that of the probation service, and also provides volunteers for the youth justice projects of social services departments in a few English counties.

Opportunities for voluntary counselling are increasingly available through prisons, and several parallel systems are in operation. Probation volunteers are often involved with prisoners, as are those recruited by SOVA. This might involve individual befriending or counselling, or co-leading groups where volunteers have appropriate skills or experience to offer. For many years, prison chaplains have also had responsibility for recruiting and supporting volunteers, who at first mainly assisted with the spiritual care of inmates. This continues, but suitably qualified chaplaincy volunteers are now increasingly helping with group work and individual counselling with prisoners. Arrangements for training and supervision vary, but the route to this kind of voluntary work invariably begins with a personal interview with the chaplain concerned. There are also opportunities in a few institutions for paid employment of a similar kind.

There are limits to the kinds of work volunteers can do. These are laid down both in the interests of protecting clients from the mistakes of unqualified people, and of preventing volunteers from taking over work that ought to be done by people who are paid for it. They also operate for the protection of volunteers, many of whom are highly enthusiastic and inclined to take on too much. For many volunteers, these constraints eventually become frustrating, and they give up or reduce their commitment to voluntary work in order to undertake counselling or social work training. Indeed, a large minority of volunteers in criminal justice offer their services precisely so as to obtain the experience necessary to take a course and begin a new career. This is nothing to be ashamed of, but agencies using volunteers understandably like to know if this is their motivation. They can then recruit a balanced volunteer group, including some with a longer-term commitment. It can be very frustrating for volunteer organizers when their best workers keep leaving for paid employment or further training!

Of course, professional staff need training too. Its availability varies considerably from one agency to another, and staff access to specific counselling training can be extremely problematic in some parts of the criminal justice system. As discussed in the next two chapters, the thrust of government policy has reduced the priority given to personal counselling in the probation service, which has been forced to concentrate upon demonstrating its efficiency, effectiveness and economy at the expense of caring for individuals. The same might be said of the police service: although police treatment of victims of crime has improved, the police are bound to concentrate upon meeting targets such as improving crime clear-up rates, often at the expense of their caring roles.

Nevertheless, some specialist training on the needs of victims is being provided. Organizations such as Victim Support and Rape Crisis teach sessions on their specialist areas of knowledge during courses for the initial and in-service training of police officers. Greater coordination between these and other criminal justice agencies is being encouraged. Police officers are increasingly trained in dealing sensitively with victims of crime, particularly if they work in specialist posts. Some feminist counselling organizations, despite trying to improve relations between themselves, their clients and the police, continue to find the attitudes of many police officers arrogant and oppressive ('T' 1988). It is counselling training as such that the police find difficult to obtain.

The initial training of probation officers has moved away from its former emphasis upon 'people skills', and many probation officers are now undertaking counselling training in addition to their basic qualifying courses. In-service training, however, is increasingly being tied to the priorities identified by area services rather than those of individual staff. This may make it harder for staff to justify the cost of specialist counselling courses: for example, a prison probation officer working with a number of men with AIDS may feel the need for training in bereavement counselling. Such training is (arguably) unlikely to be needed in generic field practice, and the officer will be working in the prison for only two or three years. In these sorts of circumstances, staff are likely to be refused funding for what they may regard as urgently needed courses. The climate is increasingly unsympathetic to counselling-style approaches to the work, with probation officers seen as 'case managers' as much as one-to-one counsellors. Their task, if clients need counselling in depth, is now seen as that of broker, finding and if necessary purchasing services to meet client needs as identified by courts. Where counselling is marginalized or discredited in this way, appropriate training becomes more difficult to obtain – and some staff have been arranging counselling courses at their own expense.

The picture is much different in the voluntary sector. Women's Aid takes a somewhat different approach from the other agencies. It does not emphasize counselling training because of the way in which the workers' and volunteers' relationship with its client group is conceptualized. Women coming for help are not described as clients, because this is seen as setting up a hierarchy, and the word counselling is avoided for similar reasons. Nevertheless, counselling skills are used informally in non-judgemental exploration of abused women's options for the future (Perry 1993).

Rape Crisis centres also see their clients as equals, but they offer counselling to help them regain control of their lives ('T' 1988), and this is 'firmly set within a social context of the oppression of women within society. Without this, it is thought that the counsellor can collude in the belief that the individual's distress is hers alone' (Perry 1993: 25). This approach has meant that the centres have been unable to rely completely upon external sources of training, many of which have been slow to respond to the insights of feminist counselling and therapy. They tend to supplement conventional basic counselling courses with their own training for staff and volunteers, drawing upon person-centred, cognitive, Gestalt and Transactional Analysis models, and emphasizing the skills needed for telephone counselling and crisis intervention. This 'in-house' training is heavily influenced by feminist ideas about the causes of male violence and about counselling itself. Because there is, as yet, no national rape crisis organization in the UK (although there is discussion of forming a national federation like the Women's Aid Federations for England, Wales and Scotland), this training has to be devised and delivered at a local level. Rape Crisis centres are also unusual in devoting a good deal of time and energy to educational work, from talks in schools and training sessions for other professionals to radio interviews, in order to raise consciousness of male violence against women. In doing so, they help to 'place the blame for rape where it should lie: on the man instead of the woman' ('T' 1988: 62).

Victim Support has the advantage of a national structure, although much of its training is also organized locally. The probation service has historically had considerable involvement in this, and schemes' training officers frequently also act as the liaison probation worker. Schemes provide a basic training for volunteers lasting three days, with only a minimal counselling component. Specialist training is increasingly being provided for volunteers and staff who counsel long-term clients, such as those who have suffered physical or sexual assaults and the survivors of murder victims.

Relate also has a national organization, and has its own college for training counsellors. Six residential courses are mandatory for new counsellors, who usually start seeing clients during this initial training under close supervision. This level of training requires a substantial commitment from counsellors, and also provides Relate with an opportunity to test their motivation and suitability rigorously. Since marriage guidance counselling is only peripherally related to the criminal justice system, it has not been discussed in detail here. Readers requiring further detail will find it in Tyndall's companion volume in this series (1993).

REWARDS OF WORKING IN CRIMINAL JUSTICE SETTINGS

Counsellors working in the criminal justice system face many obstacles, some of which are described above. They also enjoy considerable compensations when these are overcome.

The problems of clients embroiled with criminal justice agencies are often intractable and profound. They may be survivors of serious abuse, victims of crime or injustice, or perpetrators of grave crimes. Such hurts do not heal easily, and many clients resist change. When counsellors are able to assist this healing process, and to see people recovering their dignity and equilibrium, this is very satisfying. The pleasure and fulfilment involved should not be underestimated.

For some counsellors, a desire to right wrongs and make the world a better place is an important component of their motivation. Criminal justice settings provide many opportunities for this, both on the individual level in work with clients, and at a structural level. The case illustrations in this book provide a number of examples. Counselling individuals can provide chances to help people recover from the impact of crime and abuse, to escape from violent or damaging relationships, to break destructive patterns of behaviour that have led them to offend against others.

There is no doubting the satisfaction involved in seeing a client progress and change, with one's own help. Sometimes this is bound up with one's own belief system, which is perfectly acceptable as long as no manipulation, unwelcome propaganda or deception is involved. Perry (1993: 76) gives a typical example of counsellors meeting their own as well as clients' needs:

> Being at the birth of another woman's growth of confidence, assertiveness and independence, which enables her to make real choices in how she wishes to live, is so pleasing precisely *because* both client and counsellor experience oppression.

Barnes and Henessy (1995) explore this idea further, showing how a feminist therapist helped a sexually abused client begin to discover an independent identity.

Counselling can empower clients, enabling them to take up issues arising from oppression on the grounds of race, gender and disability, and a range of other questions specific to the particular setting. Prison chaplains and probation officers, for example, are challenging the prevailing assumptions about masculinity held by prisoners and staff, both in counselling individuals and in their dealings with colleagues and the prison hierarchy. Rape Crisis and Women's Aid counsellors use the insights gained in counselling to inform debate about male violence and sexual harassment. Many counsellors in criminal justice settings contribute to wider debates – about crime, the family, the treatment of offenders and victims of crime, penal policy and so on – on the basis of what they have learnt from their clients. The work with individuals may motivate the desire for social change, but it is often the other way around: counsellors become involved in helping criminal justice clients as part of their commitment to social change.

The reader may be feeling some unease at this point: the personal satisfaction involved in counselling is rarely discussed, and the types of motives discussed so far in this section may seem selfish. Counsellors should, in my view, be aware of their motivation and prepared to question the nature of the fulfilment gained from their work. An unappealing aspect of some counsellors' attraction to working with criminal justice clients is a prurient interest in offenders, prisons, policing or the drama of the courtroom. None of us is immune from this interest in secret places like prisons and police stations, and the market for 'true crime' books shows how serious crime appeals to the popular imagination, but this curiosity should never be indulged at the expense of clients' interests. Nevertheless, many counsellors will admit, if they are honest, that they enjoy their privileged access to people who have done extraordinary, deviant things and to places that are not open to people in general. This interest in people, and in unusual locations, is nothing we should be ashamed of, and it can be turned to clients' benefit. Many people's initial motivation for prison visiting is at least partly curiosity.

People drawn to counselling in criminal justice settings are vetted by the agencies using their services, either formally or informally. The volunteer training programmes are all designed to make it possible to 'counsel out' unsuitable candidates, and professional training for work in criminal justice agencies has traditionally placed great emphasis upon students' personal qualities and suitability. These requirements are not always fully explicit, and it is only when students are seen to be 'failing' that they are likely to be formulated. This can lead to unfair treatment of individual students (and of whole groups whose cultural background differs from the dominant norms), and courses training counsellors and social workers need to strive for greater clarity in this area (see Brearley 1995; Varley *et al.* 1995).

Because counselling necessarily involves supervision, and because counsellors work with a wide range of clients, part of the attraction of the work is personal development. This applies in criminal justice settings as much as elsewhere. There are also, perhaps, greater opportunities for paid employment in some of these settings than in other areas where counselling is practised and counselling skills employed – although most of the jobs do not involve the use of counselling as their main component.

Counselling in all settings raises profound questions for staff and volunteers. Why is there so much misery and injustice in the world? What is the individual's role in tackling such problems? Why are some sections of the community disproportionately victimized? Issues about our own mortality and vulnerability often arise during counselling practice. In some ways, these questions are part of the everyday work of counsellors in criminal justice settings, which makes their work demanding but stimulating and interesting. They daily struggle with the consequences of human cruelty, deviance and disorder. They work with slippery philosophical issues. When is it necessary, and when is it justified, to deprive offenders of their liberty? How can custody be made humane and dignified without making it too attractive to sentencers and recidivists? When is the commitment to client confidentiality overturned by the danger of harm to others? Those counselling in criminal justice settings are likely to be confronted by difficult questions of this kind. It is important that they are prepared for this. While particular dilemmas cannot always be anticipated, training needs to reflect the likelihood that dealing with the criminal justice system is likely to throw up its fair share of such problems (perhaps by including role play exercises using scenarios such as the case illustrations included in the present volume).

There are positive and negative aspects of the moral and philosophical questioning carried out by counsellors in criminal justice. Sometimes they might prefer to get on with the job, and sometimes the pressure of work is too great to allow proper consideration of important issues. Nevertheless, criminal justice settings are invariably interesting and intellectually stimulating places to work because they do constantly require consideration of such questions. This encourages practitioners' personal growth, as long as they have adequate supervision and support to allow them to explore the ethical implications of their work.

Some of the settings described in this book also offer counsellors opportunities to work in considerable depth, which provides not only an intellectual challenge but also great scope for personal development and for the client to change. Counsellors can thus gain several different types of satisfaction from such work. Perry (1993: 85) notes that 'other workers often envy counsellors', and this is true in several criminal justice agencies. Many counsellors in these agencies have considerable freedom and many opportunities to work innovatively and intensively with clients. Prison chaplains, for example, enjoy a privileged position in terms of their autonomy and the scope it gives them for creative work with individual clients and groups (see Chapter Three). They are also free to remain detached from the institutional hierarchy and, to a certain extent, they are in a position to be critical in public of the institution of imprisonment. They have some say over the regime of the prisons they work in, and the potential to influence things for the better. Few counsellors have such freedom and power at work!

Similarly, counsellors working in campaigning agencies have considerable scope for activism, to try to influence policies and attitudes outside their workplace. Rape Crisis counsellors are invariably involved in educational work as well as individual counselling, and the same applies to a lesser extent to those involved in Victim Support. The staff and volunteers in these agencies also have autonomy in respect of their individual clients: they receive advice and support in supervision, but ultimately the important decisions are theirs. They can choose the model and methods to be used with each client, and they do not have to keep detailed records.

Despite the requirements of increasingly managerialist styles of supervision, workers in statutory agencies also retain a certain amount of autonomy in these respects. Senior staff are unlikely to stipulate which methods probation officers should use with individual clients – although they may make it difficult for the main-grade officers to work in depth with more than a small number of individuals. The senior probation officers' role of allocating the work among the members of teams puts them in a powerful position, and it is increasingly difficult to sustain long-term counselling with more than a few clients. All the same, probation officers have far more discretion than many staff at comparable levels in other criminal justice agencies, such as the Crown Prosecution Service or the prison service.

What all counsellors in criminal justice have in common is their ability to influence the practice of others. Some aspects of this have been considered earlier in this section, but it is worth highlighting the existence of the various codes of ethics and the more informal consensus about values generated by counselling practice. Brearley (1995) lucidly discusses the overlaps between the British Association of Counselling's code of ethics and that of the British Association of Social Workers. Although many of the staff involved in counselling in British criminal justice settings belong to neither of these organizations, the great majority do subscribe to almost every detail of the codes of ethics. Those involved in counselling (and those using counselling skills) in criminal justice settings have been enormously influential in terms of the evolution of these codes of practice and in defining good practice in their own particular fields. I would argue that this ability to influence the practice of others, and to help to define what ethical practice involves, is a particularly satisfying aspect of working in criminal justice counselling.

A recent example was discussed earlier in this chapter. When the Home Office introduced the Victim's Charter, it failed to take note of the objections raised by probation organizations and the National Association of Victim Support Schemes. The provision whereby probation officers would be expected to contact the surviving family members of murder victims, usually many years after the offence, was retained. Early examples of practice in this area were so alarming in terms of their adverse effects upon survivors that the organizations got together to work out better ways of responding. The Home Office ultimately issued a circular that condoned probation officers' decision not to implement the policy retrospectively, and to do so selectively where more recent offences were concerned.

Probation officers and Victim Support schemes had direct experience of the damage that was being done by a policy that was arguably devised and introduced primarily for publicity purposes (Kosh and Williams 1995). It was unethical to use clients in this way, and neither the probation service nor local Victim Support schemes anyway had the resources to prepare and counsel clients properly. In the end, policy was changed as a result of counsellors' refusal to compromise on matters of principle.

Such examples could doubtless be found in other areas of counselling, but it does seem that a particular satisfaction of working in criminal justice settings is that there is a degree of consensus about what comprises ethical practice. Counsellors in these settings are willing to take personal risks to ensure that such principles are not compromised, and they have found mechanisms for cooperating to bring the consensus into their practice. It does not always happen as quickly as in this example, but the readiness to tackle such issues makes criminal justice settings more invigorating and optimistic places to work.

The issues of cooperation and the relationships between different professions form the core of the next chapter. What can the different agencies do to improve working relationships between them, and how appropriate are the existing efforts to defend the boundaries erected between different professions working in criminal justice? How do such 'turf wars' impinge upon the quality of counselling practice? The chapter concludes by returning to the question of 'what works' in the counselling of offenders, victims of crime and criminal justice professionals and volunteers in more general terms.

· FIVE ·

Professional relationships in counselling in criminal justice

An important part of the work of those who aim to help offenders and the victims of crime is in making connections between the different parts of the criminal justice system. Offenders and victims often need information about how the system works, what rights and entitlements they have, and whom to talk to about what. Better inter-agency liaison by social work and criminal justice agencies has been advocated in official reports and policies in many different contexts (Raynor *et al.* 1994; Brearley 1995; Kosh and Williams 1995), but effective work of this kind involves overcoming barriers between different professions and transcending the often substantial cultural differences between agencies. In practice, these can prove to be formidable obstacles, but counselling skills are helpful in avoiding them.

The existing relationships between the different parts of the criminal justice system (however strained) also offer an opportunity to 'sell' counselling interventions in appropriate circumstances to colleagues in partner agencies, although they may initially be sceptical. Effective work can influence future referrals and thus benefit clients, so this is a promising and rewarding area of endeavour. There are dangers, though, and the boundaries of professional relationships with clients need to be carefully defined so as not to breach trust when communication occurs between agencies with different values and priorities.

PROFESSIONAL BOUNDARIES

There are significant differences in the ways various criminal justice agencies approach particular situations. The different interpretations of the notion of professional boundaries provide an interesting example. The Samaritans have recently become involved in preventing suicide and self-harm among prisoners. As an agency, Samaritans clearly insist upon confidentiality. Where other agencies may only pay lip service to clients' right to a confidential service, Samaritans jealously protect the identity and other details of their staff, volunteers and clients – and make no exceptions (Varah 1980: 79). This rigid adherence to an important principle of counselling raises eyebrows in agencies that are accustomed to sharing information about clients much more liberally, although they claim to espouse social work values. Thus, when the Samaritans, first in Boston, Massachusetts, and later in Wales, became involved in the prevention of suicides and self-harm in prisons, they would not compromise on the principle of confidentiality, and their invitation to assist with the problem was opposed by many prison staff. Prison officers in particular saw them as 'outsiders, encroaching on our territory' and likely to compromise security (Davies 1994: 133).

The involvement of the Samaritans at Swansea Prison was very carefully managed, and they trained prisoners and staff to act as 'listeners', offering them confidential supervision inside the prison once a week. The prison's suicide and self-injury rate fell dramatically, and the scheme spread within three years to over 60 other prisons (Davies 1994; *Life Support* 1995). Those involved in the scheme claimed that the project built up a relationship of considerable trust between the local Samaritans and prison staff. Indeed, some of the traditional but inhumane methods of dealing with suicidal prisoners were questioned by the people involved in the project, and the prison environment and regime were improved in response to their suggestions.

A contrasting example of the treatment of confidential information is the unprofessional way in which the details of prisoners' offences – and even their medical diagnoses – are discussed among uniformed prison staff. For some years, until the practice was criticized in the Woolf Report and increasingly by penal reform groups, information about prisoners with infectious diseases was actually written on their cell doors, with predictable consequences in terms of victimization and ostracism by other inmates (Padel 1995). One would have expected staff commitment to medical ethics to have prevented such abuse of information collected within the context of a confidential doctor–patient relationship, but professional ethics can become corrupted within 'total institutions'. In this instance, it appears that the medical profession agreed to a Home Office suggestion that the doctor–patient relationship can legitimately be extended to include some uniformed prison officers on a 'need-to-know basis', a policy that seems more in the interests of expedience than of patient care (Thomas 1994). Until the late 1980s, the chalking of a crude code on cell doors was seen as an acceptable way of disguising the information that particular individuals were HIV positive or had other infectious illnesses.

Similar policies have been followed in other jurisdictions, for example in Canada, but subsequently reversed as a result of prisoners taking cases to court (Jurgens 1994). Even in countries with comparatively liberal penal policies, the confidentiality of prisoners' seropositivity has been routinely compromised (as in Norway (Scherdin 1994) and the Netherlands (Moerings 1994)).

Counsellors in criminal justice settings also have occasion to work with another uniformed service, the police. Like the prison service, their priorities often do not encourage them to display much sympathy towards counselling: they want offenders convicted and locked up, and they have not always shown much more concern for the human needs of victims of crime. There have been considerable changes in the latter respect over the last two decades, as a result of the work of Victim Support, officially endorsed and increasingly funded by the probation service (Kosh and Williams 1995). Nevertheless, many victims of crime still find the police insensitive to their plight and more focused on offenders. They complain that the police fail to keep them informed (although it is government policy that victims should be told at various stages what is happening to 'their' offender), and that no specific provision is made for their needs when they have to give evidence in court.

Initiatives are being taken to address these concerns, but the police are bound to be more concerned with criminals than victims under the existing system, where their efficiency is measured largely in terms of the numbers of offenders caught and processed. Some police officers, however, do specialize in areas of work that involve the use of counselling skills, particularly those dealing with survivors of sexual assault and family violence. This can raise particular difficulties and conflicts, which were discussed in Chapter Three.

INTER-AGENCY RELATIONS

For counselling agencies, the kind of abuse suffered by clients at the hands of the prison service and sometimes the police poses real difficulties about involvement in inter-agency work. Many uniformed staff in prisons do the work from the best of motives, and when they engage in 'welfare' work alongside psychologists, teachers, chaplains and probation officers, they begin to understand and espouse the underlying principles of caring work. For quite understandable reasons, however, the prisoners are unwilling to trust them. The custodial staff's prime concern is security, and with the best will in the world, they cannot treat confidentiality (or respect for persons) as principles that override the need to keep prisoners inside. Collusion with physical abuse of the kind discussed in Chapter Three may be an extreme example, but there will always be conflicts on matters of principle between custodial and care staff in total institutions. Recorded information is vulnerable not only to disclosure by staff acting unprofessionally, but also, in the prison environment, to unauthorized access.

Pursuing this argument in a wider context, it is clear that conflicts of this kind arise for all those trying to bridge the gap between counselling and criminal justice. There is a crisis of legitimacy, a lack of confidence in the criminal justice system in general, and widespread doubts about the legitimacy of the prison system in particular (Cavadino and Dignan 1992; Sparks 1994), in most English-speaking countries (which have historically tended to favour policies that involve incarcerating high proportions of their offenders). The legitimacy of these prison systems is increasingly being challenged because the dominance of a certain kind of white, male, macho culture in the prisons is no longer generally acceptable (see Chapter Two; for a discussion of police legitimacy see Fielding (1994)). On an optimistic note, it is the outside, counselling-orientated professionals who are challenging this culture, with some effect. Probation officers and chaplains in particular have raised questions about the efficacy of militaristic, macho methods of working with prisoners. In a few prisons, they have begun to run men's groups and to raise gender issues in other client groups and in the course of staff training.

Chaplains based in prisons are increasingly taking up opportunities to train as counsellors, and over a third of them have at least basic training. As psychologists are driven into concentrating on risk assessment and psychological testing, and probation staff into putting large numbers of clients through group work programmes, chaplains have been able to redefine their functions and move into this area of work. While their traditional role was perhaps an inherently judgemental one, they now largely eschew this in favour of individual work aimed at helping clients towards wholeness and insight. All these 'civilian' staff working in prison have a responsibility to liaise constructively with each other in the interests of clients, and they increasingly work together in an effort to influence the ethos and regimes of individual prisons.

There are profound ideological and ethical differences between the underlying values of counselling and those of imprisonment (see Williams 1995a). In these circumstances, the need for clarity about the boundaries between care and control, and between those who exercise each function, is obvious. Unfortunately, there is no clear demarcation in terms of professional functions. Prison-based social workers, for example, carry keys. Police officers, as we have seen in Chapter Two, see a large part of their work as analogous to social work, despite the low prestige of such aspects of policing. Social workers of all kinds have a range of controlling functions as well as their counselling roles, varying in degree according to the settings in which they work. For this reason, workers and volunteers cannot operate on the basis of crude rules of thumb: they need to understand and test the value base of their own organization and occupational group. For professional staff in particular, this needs to involve adequate exposure to ethical issues during initial training – although this is controversial in the current political climate in the UK (Barnett 1994).

It is, in any case, inevitable that cultural differences between organizations will act as a constraint upon effective communication between them. Each partner in inter-agency work tends to bring preconceptions, which affect communications:

> different agencies effectively speak different languages: they have different cognitive frameworks, different assumptive worlds, and different discourses. Thus, whatever the analysis of the problem might say, agencies will seek solutions which square with their own conceptions.
>
> (Gilling 1994: 251)

Recognizing this, staff exchanges have been set up to try to reduce dysfunctional communication of this kind, and some inter-professional training has also helped to address the problem (Brearley 1995), although this is unlikely to be sufficient where there is no regular, reflective, professional supervision available to staff in their 'home' agencies (Woodhouse and Pengelly 1991).

Individuals can also overcome communication problems by using their own networks. In an interesting study that appears to have been an unexpected outcome of research into inter-agency working in criminal justice, Sampson *et al.* (1991) have shown how women can transcend agency boundaries in the interests of their shared clients by simply ignoring the conventional hierarchies and protocols that are meant to regulate communications between the police and the social and probation services. Feeling marginalized by discrimination and sexual harassment at work, and experiencing the police in general as a difficult agency with which to liaise, women in social and probation services found sympathetic female colleagues in the police and communicated directly with them. Such networking seems likely to have benefited clients without subjecting staff to unnecessary stress.

In some areas, individual relationships transcend other kinds of formal boundaries to communication between criminal justice agencies. Although Victim Support schemes mainly concentrate upon short-term, practical help for victims of crime, they do also increasingly engage in counselling people whose reaction to victimization is more extreme. In urban areas, the police tend to filter referrals to Victim Support schemes in order to try to avoid deluging Victim Support coordinators with trivial matters. In some counties, schemes have resisted this on the grounds that the nature of the offence is not a good predictor of the severity of the victim's reaction. The national Victim Support body has encouraged scheme coordinators to instal fax machines so that all offences with personal victims can be referred quickly. In at least one rural area, coordinators have resisted this on the grounds that personal contact with a trusted colleague in the police is a much more effective way of judging which victims are likely to need longer-term help than any amount of faxed official information.

Barriers to communication between agencies may be erected deliberately, which is probably sometimes the position in the case of the police, but they can also arise from differences of agency cultures. The insights of counsellors can be profoundly helpful in showing members of different agencies what it is that is hindering effective liaison: Brearley (1995: 118–19) gives a number of examples of what she calls 'process consultancy'. The outsider trained in counselling can often neutralize or bring into the open inter-agency conflicts and tackle impediments to progress in a way that people inside the agencies are unable to do. Understanding of the dynamics of groups can also be invaluable in challenging 'entrenched agency or professional defences' (Woodhouse and Pengelly 1991: 8). This will normally happen only where agency staff are aware of the problem and sympathetic to counselling as a solution. It can be a powerful influence for change where the organizational culture allows this. Some prison governors encourage their psychologist colleagues to see themselves as consultants on issues of group process during management meetings, and similar alliances might be formed between psychologists, chaplains and probation staff where conditions allowed.

Where agencies are working in partnership, power differentials can get in the way of effective cooperation. This is a particular problem when the weaker partner is trying to represent the interests of 'relatively powerless and often unrepresented minority groups' (Sampson *et al.* 1988: 485) and the more powerful agency sees such groups as peripheral to its main mission. In such situations, the large, statutory organizations are often in a position to set the policy agenda and they tend to marginalize issues that minority groups would see as central (Kosh and Williams 1995). While counselling skills may be of little help in altering such power differentials, counsellors have an important role in trying to empower minority groups and in helping the dominant groups to consider other perspectives. In this context, the minority group might be a new black voluntary agency, such as those that have been set up to support the partners of black, male prisoners; or it might be a well established and thriving local Victim Support scheme. Both have to find their way around the bureaucracy involved in obtaining funding through the probation service. The statutory agency's staff need to understand the voluntary agency's perspective and culture, and vice versa.

It is possible in practice for counsellors to work within apparently hostile host agencies and uphold professional values. Tyndall (1993: 23) gives the example of Catholic marriage guidance counsellors working in non-directive ways within a specifically Catholic agency, 'which resulted in the thrust of their counselling often being at variance with the Church's official line, particularly on contraception'. As a result of such a process, some unexpected alliances are likely to be formed, as colleagues and clients see the benefits of counselling and come to understand its value base. Similarly, the struggle over the values of the probation service in England and Wales in the 1990s has been between politicians with a particular view of the efficacy of punishment, and a counselling-influenced preference among practitioners for more humane ways of changing offenders' behaviour for the better. The criminal justice system may be inherently coercive, but this does not mean that probation officers need be predominantly directive in their practice. Indeed, non-directive work built upon trusting personal relationships is likely to be more effective, a nuance which is clearly too subtle for some of the politicians taking simplistic public positions on these issues.

Counsellors' understanding of professional and personal defences and values is invaluable in avoiding the pitfalls of oversimplified distinctions such as that between 'care' and 'control' in probation practice. It also helps to put some of the inter-agency conflicts and misunderstandings discussed earlier into a proper context (see Woodhouse and Pengelly (1991) for a fascinating discussion of the psychological mechanisms involved in interactions between probation officers and colleagues in other agencies).

Similarly, prison chaplains can sometimes ask questions and make suggestions that encourage governors and others in positions of authority to reflect upon the moral basis of their decision making. They can – and do – also act as the grit in the machine of the prison bureaucracy when they feel that it is rolling along too smoothly (Shaw 1995).

This is not to suggest that trained counsellors and social workers can simply pass their skills on to other staff and volunteers by example, or that it is easy to help others to apply the insights gained by professional training. The 'sitting next to Nellie' model of training, whereby trainees are expected to absorb expertise simply by watching a skilled practitioner at work, clearly does not apply to complex and sophisticated skills of the kind used by caring professionals in criminal justice. In practice, this means that some work has to be reserved for trained staff, and ways have to be found to avoid exposing clients to the risks involved in allowing unqualified workers and volunteers to exceed their legitimate brief.

PRESSURES ON CRIMINAL JUSTICE AGENCIES

Unfortunately, there is a tendency in hard-pressed public-sector agencies to try to cut corners for financial reasons, using insufficiently trained workers to deliver sophisticated treatment. The example of the prison Sex Offender Treatment Programme, discussed in greater detail in Chapter Two, is a case in point. Psychologists and probation officers were expected to work alongside uniformed staff in groups of convicted sexual offenders, trying to persuade them to change their behaviour and the cognitive processes leading up to it. All the programme staff had attended a brief training course, but it did nothing to encourage them to address questions about their own sexuality or their values relating to illegal sexual behaviour. For many of the prison officers, it was their first experience of any kind of training in the psychology of sexual offending or in offender treatment.

The other professions, not wishing to seem precious about their qualifications, or to prejudice the implementation of a large-scale treatment programme, went along with the idea that groups would be co-led with unqualified staff. In many cases, the uniformed staff were highly motivated and had a great deal to offer as group leaders, and professional colleagues gave informal support and supervision. It is nevertheless very unfortunate that prison officers began their involvement in offender rehabilitation in such an inauspicious way. It says a great deal about the prison service's attitude to them that they were put in such an invidious position.

When it came to co-leading the groups, the respective workers' roles had to be clarified. While prisoners would respect the views of psychologists about different forms of treatment, and the views of probation officers about the workings of the early release system, prison officers had a role in discussions about therapeutic regimes at other prisons and about likely punishments for infractions of institutional rules. It was important for the staff to show that they could work harmoniously together, and for them to respect the professional expertise each brought to the group. To achieve this, some negotiation had to take place outside the group itself, and staff had to put time into discussion and thinking about the process of the group. Unfortunately, this work was not always formally recognized by the prison service as being necessary, and it was thus difficult to find the time to do it properly.

Outside the group, offenders needed support in thinking about and dealing with what they were learning about themselves. Prison officers had to be aware of their own limitations, assisting where possible, but referring men to qualified colleagues when circumstances suggested this.

Similarly, there are issues about the degree of involvement in personal counselling that it is appropriate for volunteers to undertake. In the probation service, the trade unions have negotiated formal agreements outlining 'role boundaries' between the work appropriate for volunteers and unqualified and professional staff. In smaller and voluntary organizations, these boundaries can become blurred, and it is questionable whether this should be tolerated in view of the risks to which clients and the public can become exposed. Volunteers in some agencies (such as Victim Support) may wish to be involved with clients only at a practical, relatively undemanding level (see case illustration 2.4). On some occasions, however, there may be a temptation for volunteers to take on inappropriate levels of involvement, and this is where a shared understanding of boundaries is important.

Case illustration 5.1

Rose is referred to Victim Support for assistance following an assault in a subway. She is an intelligent single woman of 59, who nursed her mother until her death six years ago with Alzheimer's disease. Since then, Rose has suffered depression and feelings of guilt, often using alcohol and prescribed medication, and has given up her job.

Lesley is the volunteer asked to work with Rose. She has a certificate in counselling, and has been with Victim Support for two years. The scheme gives her what information it has – that Rose is retired, that her mother died six years ago and the circumstances in which she was assaulted.

Lesley visits Rose armed with a criminal injuries compensation form. On this first visit, she finds Rose very depressed, and ends up staying with her for four hours. She sees this as her first opportunity to do what she sees as 'real counselling', and jumps at the chance. She leaves a message for the scheme coordinator saying that she will visit Rose again the next day, and begins to do so regularly. Rose seems very grateful and often says how much Lesley's visits have helped her.

After some weeks, Rose discloses that she is having suicidal feelings, and asks Lesley to stay the night with her. Instead, Lesley decides to give Rose her home telephone number, although this is explicitly discouraged during Victim Support volunteer training. A few days later she receives a telephone call from Rose at 4.00 a.m. saying that she has taken an overdose, and goes to her home to take her to hospital. Next day she tries to encourage Rose to talk to her general practitioner, but she refuses, saying that Lesley's help is all she needs. Lesley feels she can handle the situation, and gives only routine reports to the Victim Support coordinator about Rose.

On a future visit when Rose, who has been drinking, verbally abuses Lesley, she realizes that things are going badly wrong. She feels overwhelmed by Rose's demands and shocked at the way she is being treated. Only then does she discuss the matter with her supervisor, and it is possible to extricate herself from the relationship only with great difficulty and support from Victim Support. Months later, when Lesley reads in the local paper that Rose has been convicted of shoplifting, she feels somehow responsible. She feels guilty about 'abandoning' Rose and not being able to solve her problems. She begins to doubt her ability to offer appropriate support, and decides to take a break from seeing clients.

In this case, the volunteer gradually blurs the boundaries between friendship and counselling instead of using them to protect herself and the client. A proper structure is available to support her, but she fails to use it until almost too late. In such circumstances, it is very difficult for voluntary agencies to hold their counsellors accountable: they are, after all, volunteers giving their own time. Constraints on resources can make it difficult to offer detailed supervision on every case, and paid coordinators tend to take on difficult-looking cases themselves rather than allocating them to volunteers, which can in turn reduce the availability of supervision further. Any experienced counsellor would recognize the process of overinvolvement and 'rescuing', but Lesley does not tell her supervisor all she needs to know in order to make such an assessment.

Victims of crime may be particularly likely to excite counsellors' rescuing instincts, but so are many offenders (and indeed, many offenders are also themselves criminally victimized). Counsellors working with these client groups need regular, professional supervision. They also need preparatory training that emphasizes not only the need for appropriate boundaries in counselling, but also why this is important. It is one thing to tell people what is expected in particular situations; a far more powerful tool is training that uses realistic case material in role play.

A difficulty faced by those attempting to employ counselling skills in criminal justice settings is that they, unlike most of their counterparts in private practice, are subject to the constraints of working in bureaucratic, hierarchical organizations. In such bureaucracies, people's understanding of accountability is likely to involve an assumption that the first loyalty of the professional worker should be to the agency, and that the interests of the client or the wider profession should come some way further down the list of priorities. This difficulty has been exacerbated by political developments over the last two decades: what has been called (in a ghastly but descriptive neologism) the 'managerialization' of the public sector has been driven by 'new right' political imperatives (Newman and Clarke 1994: 25). Professions are seen as too powerful and as insensitive to the overriding need for market-driven efficiency. The solution imposed is to empower managers in the public sector at the expense of professional power, a process that has taken different forms in the various parts of the criminal justice system. Prison governors and senior police officers have arguably been transformed from professionals to bureaucratic managers, while front-line workers like probation officers have been increasingly expected to act as 'case managers' rather than concentrating upon direct service to clients (Humphrey *et al.* 1993; Simiç 1995).

The implications for the place of counselling within the criminal justice system are fairly obvious: it has been marginalized. Paradoxically, this has meant that many professionals have become much more aware of what they are in danger of losing, and many probation officers, for example, have decided to remain as main-grade staff and avoid promotion to wholly bureaucratic posts (while others, particularly black people and women, have been effectively excluded from promotion by the dominant ideology: see Flynn (1995)). The probation service has traditionally found ways of making the best of externally imposed change, somehow incorporating it into the dominant ethos, which is one sympathetic to offender counselling and group work rather than to mechanistic surveillance.

Ever since the 1970s, however, probation officers have worked within bureacracies (Beaumont 1995), and this has always provided scope for conflict and misunderstandings. The criminal justice system does not in fact really work as a system, despite the general use of this short-hand phrase, and within each of its constituent agencies there are different working definitions even of such basic concepts as justice itself (Ward 1995). With the exception of prison psychology departments and specialist forensic psychiatry services, which both employ relatively small numbers of staff, the probation service is the main home of counselling skills and values within criminal justice agencies. It upholds these in a variety of ways: its commitment to non-judgemental ways of working, and to equal opportunities, have always brought it into conflict with other parts of the system. The imposition of managerialism has created new conflicts within the probation service, and set the scene for more frequent conflict too between probation officers and other bureaucracy-based professionals (Humphrey *et al.* 1993).

Case illustration 5.2

Under the national standards governing probation work (Home Office 1995), Phil is required as the supervising probation officer to return clients to court for non-compliance if they miss a specified number of appointments within a particular period. Marcus is a young, single cannabis user who is halfway through a probation order, supervised by Phil. He leads a disorganized life, moving from one temporary address to another quite frequently and is constantly in difficulties with his benefit claims. He calls in at the probation office fairly often for help in dealing with his accommodation and money problems – but rarely remembers to keep specific appointments, and usually sees whoever is on duty rather than Phil himself. His offending is minor (possession of small quantities of soft drugs) but continual. Phil does not feel that there is much scope for one-to-one work, but believes that the probation order provides Marcus with general support and a sense of stability, and sees him as presenting no risk to himself or others.

Phil's supervision plan for Marcus (which he is required by the national standards to write and review) sets out the purpose and desired outcome of the probation order mainly in terms of actually getting Marcus through the order without him breaching it or reoffending. It requires fortnightly contact, but Marcus has been out of touch for nearly three weeks. This has happened twice before, and a plausible explanation was subsequently provided. Under the terms of the standards, formal written warnings had to be issued about the earlier breaches, and Phil now has no further discretion: he has to initiate court proceedings within 10 days of the third breach of the order.

Although breaches have become more common since national standards were introduced, courts have not all changed their sentencing habits. In Phil's area, any breach action is likely to lead to imprisonment. He feels badly about taking such action against Marcus, but has little choice. What relationship Marcus had with the probation service is unlikely to survive a period of imprisonment for breaching the order.

In this case bureaucratic constraints, which were imposed to encourage the probation service to be more severe with clients who do not fully comply with the conditions of supervision, are in danger of making effective supervision impossible. The courts, taking literally the pronouncements of politicians about 'getting tough', are in danger of excluding relatively minor offenders from the benefits of counselling under the terms of probation orders if they lead disorganized lives and fail to comply with bureaucratically defined disciplinary measures.

Case illustration 5.3

Mary is a Midlands probation officer with a small caseload of serious offenders. She receives a letter from Jo, a life sentence prisoner currently serving her time in Durham. Jo is seriously depressed, and asks her to visit as soon as possible. Mary rings the senior probation officer at the prison to say that she would like to make a visit, which is overdue anyway according to her supervision plan, agreed with Jo at the start of her sentence, but financial restrictions mean she can make no more prison visits outside the immediate area for the next six weeks. The prison-based colleague agrees to talk to Jo, and rings Mary later in the day to confirm that she is having suicidal feelings and has been transferred to the prison's hospital wing.

Mary arranges to speak to Jo on the telephone, but her senior officer tells her she has to make a case in writing through the line management system to obtain permission to visit. She decides to tell Jo she is coming and argue about the expenses later. It will in any case be over a week before she has a day free to make the visit.

When they do meet, 10 days later, Mary is glad she did not go by the book. She is able to cement her relationship with Jo by helping her to see that she has deep-rooted problems, which she wants to work on while she is in prison, and agrees to write in support of her request to be transferred to a prison nearer home so that they can begin this work together. Meanwhile, she gets Jo's permission to disclose the background to the depression to her colleague at the prison, who is able to join them for a few minutes at the end of the visit.

This case shows that professionals who are confident about what they have to offer and about championing clients' needs can overcome bureaucratic hurdles imposed by their agencies. In practice, however, there is a limit to the number of occasions on which staff are allowed to circumvent rules that are designed to limit demand (and expenditure). Mary will probably have another case to argue when it comes to engaging in counselling with Jo over more than quite a short period: not only will the travelling expenses to even a local prison have to be justified, but the time involved will also have to be protected. In such circumstances, there is a temptation to avoid committing oneself to working in any depth with imprisoned clients, and to give in to the demands of the bureaucracy (Williams 1992b).

In more and more such cases, staff who are trained in counselling are having to consider themselves rather as case managers (Day 1995; Simiç 1995). They may have formed a relationship with an individual client, on which they feel they can helpfully build, but other demands on their time and on agency resources necessitate referral to specialist agencies. Depending on the exact nature of Jo's difficulties, she might be referred for counselling to a Rape Crisis centre or to a psychologist or probation officer within the prison.

This kind of difficulty can impinge upon the outside agencies in all kinds of ways. The few groups that exist to provide counselling for women, for example, are faced with difficult decisions about priorities if they accept referrals from agencies such as probation. Jo has no income, and is unlikely to receive help from anywhere else – but Rape Crisis centres frequently have no secure funding, and cannot survive if they become unduly committed to relieving hard-pressed, but reasonably well funded, statutory agencies of their clients. It may be possible for the probation service to devote part of its budget to assisting such agencies in its area, but they then become obliged to keep statistics on the number of probation clients assisted, which necessitates asking people intrusive questions at a sensitive time.

GENERIC COUNSELLORS AND CRIMINAL JUSTICE

Although some counsellors may never work with clients who are in contact with the criminal justice system, a surprising number find themselves occasionally confronted with questions and ethical dilemmas arising from such contact. I cannot hope to cover all possible eventualities in this section, but it may be of interest to review some such cases and reflect upon their possible implications. (I am very grateful to two groups of counselling students at Keele University for their help in generating this case material, the details of which have been altered in the interests of confidentiality.)

Even people who work in one part of the criminal justice system may find that their ability to practise effectively as a counsellor is diminished by a client's removal to another. The obvious example is the client who is imprisoned.

Case illustration 5.4

Audrey was a Victim Support volunteer who had undertaken advanced training and was involved in long-term counselling with a small number of clients. When she received a referral to visit a new client in a women's prison, she was initially apprehensive.

The client, Tracey, had been raped a few days before she was imprisoned in an unrelated case. She very much welcomed the offer of confidential counselling, but this was difficult to sustain when other prisoners (who on Audrey's first arrival were sunbathing on the grass outside) expressed interest in the reasons for her visits each time Audrey arrived on the house block. After a while, she and Tracey agreed a 'cover story'.

Tracey also asked a number of questions about the workings of the prison system that Audrey felt she did not begin to know how to answer. Some issues were passed on, with Tracey's permission, to be discussed with a prison probation officer, who also agreed to spend some time with Audrey talking in general terms about the effects of imprisonment. Although Audrey confessed in supervision that she initially felt she was 'in deep water', the case began to have more in common with others she had dealt with than she had expected. The prison environment introduced some unfamiliar constraints – such as Tracey's unavailability for one appointment because of a family visit unexpectedly occurring at the same time, and her tendency at other times to want to chat at length about her home town because she knew hardly anyone else who came from there – but Audrey began to feel experienced at dealing with these. (She waited, reading a newspaper, until after Tracey's family had completed their visit, and later gave them a lift to the station; she subsequently sent Tracey the local paper to keep her in touch with events.)

In this case, the counsellor is used to dealing with clients in criminal justice settings such as courts, but feels some concern about how she will cope with the prison as a context for her work. In practice, she is able to use the resources available to her (the relationship with the client, her supervisor, the probation officer, and indeed her car) and soon feels relatively at home counselling in the new environment.

Case illustration 5.5

Jeff is a counsellor for a drug and alcohol counselling agency. He is asked to work with Martin, a young man living in a hostel funded by a voluntary agency, because of a drug-related offence. The hostel warden arranges for them to meet in her office for an hour one evening a week after Martin gets in from work, but there are problems about privacy and Jeff finds it difficult to make best use of a weekly, time-limited interview when his concentration is broken by interruptions.

He feels he has made a good start with Martin, who is highly motivated, and they agree to ask if future appointments can be at the drug agency's office. Although the warden offers to arrange for Martin's bedroom to be unlocked for the weekly counselling sessions, Jeff stands his ground and says that he does not think this would be appropriate. It is agreed that the warden will apply for a variation of Martin's bail conditions, and counselling resumes in the relative calm of Jeff's office.

In the prison setting, counsellors sometimes simply have to make the best of a difficult environment. Elsewhere in the criminal justice system, it may at times be necessary to stand up for clients' rights to privacy and confidentiality. Diplomatic liaison with staff of other agencies will often be needed.

Counsellors in all settings are likely to come across the occasional client who has been charged with or witnessed an offence, or been the victim of one. They may have common-sense assumptions about the criminal justice system that are challenged by their clients' experiences. For example, Jenkins (1994) describes the case of a counsellor who supported a client through the disclosure and reporting to the police of a rape. Innocent attempts to help the client through a criminal trial can be characterized by defence lawyers as 'coaching' a potential witness, and the very existence of the counselling relationship has on occasions been used to suggest that the complainant is in some way unstable and her evidence therefore unreliable. A counsellor who 'had previously seen the law as being a neutral or benign force' (Jenkins 1994: 49) discovered that this is not necessarily the case. In future, this knowledge can be used to prepare clients for the ordeal of a criminal trial, and perhaps in some cases protect them from the worst excesses of barristers' tactics. This issue is discussed in further detail in Chapter Six.

Of course, contact with the criminal justice system may be unavoidable if clients' best interests are to be served. The counsellor in the case Jenkins describes might have been well advised to discuss the case with an experienced Rape Crisis or Victim Support worker or a probation officer before attending court. Victim Support has campaigned for better provision for witnesses and complainants at court (Victim Support 1995), but counsellors need to be thoroughly prepared if they are to be effective in helping clients in unfamiliar settings. Otherwise, there is a danger that clients will feel let down: counsellors may be excellent practitioners, in command of the theory and practice of counselling people who have suffered loss, but they also need to be able to support the client through potentially bruising contact with the courts and the police.

Case illustration 5.6

Jessica's daughter was murdered eight years ago. She has been seeing an experienced bereavement counsellor, Bill, for much of the time since her daughter's death. Although this has been some help, she felt disappointed that Bill knew little about the series of shocks Jessica and her family were to receive over the eight years. The police had been very supportive at the time, but their contact gradually tailed off. She then made contact with Bill, and he was very helpful, but a series of crises for Jessica seemed to come as a surprise to Bill as well as to her.

First, by the time the murderer was brought to trial, 18 months had passed since the offence. Jessica and her husband attended court, and a variety of unpleasant details of her daughter's death were disclosed for the first time, setting her grieving process back.

Then, the convicted offender appealed against his sentence, and there was another distressing trial. Just over seven years after the death, the police got in touch to say that the convicted man was now being considered for parole. A few months later, a probation officer wrote to ask for an appointment to discuss the possibility of the offender eventually returning to live in the area.

Just before that, Jessica happened to read in the newspaper about the work of a group called Support After Murder and Manslaughter (SAMM, which can be contacted through Victim Support). She was put in touch with local people who had undergone experiences similar to hers and her husband's, and she found out more about how the criminal justice system affects people in their circumstances. After a while, she became active in helping other bereaved parents and in campaigning for changes to the system. She discovered that more than one member of the local SAMM group was undertaking counselling training, aiming to increase counsellors' awareness of the issues as well as to help other people in a similar position.

Self-help groups like SAMM have considerable experience and a great willingness to help others. There is a rather patronizing tendency among criminal justice professionals to steer people clear of such organizations in case they come to some harm at their hands. Sometimes, members of self-help groups know far more about the workings and effects of the criminal justice system than the professionals who work within it, and they should be given due credit for this.

WHAT WORKS IN COUNSELLING OFFENDERS

Counsellors have not always been as concerned as other helping professionals to demonstrate the effectiveness of their intervention: in much of the literature, the benefits of counselling seem to be taken for granted. A worthwhile human relationship between counsellor and client is good in itself. While this is doubtless true, there is increasing pressure – particularly, but not solely, upon those working in the public sector – to demonstrate the value of counselling in terms of positive outcomes.

An important element in the success of counselling is the degree of optimism the counsellors feel about the likelihood of a beneficial outcome. This will influence results in individual cases and also more generally. Counselling is practised, and counselling skills employed, in such a wide variety of ways and settings that it is not easy to generalize about its effectiveness. Evidence is available, though, of successes in certain specific areas, and some of this is reviewed below.

Before considering this research, some questions of methodology need brief consideration. The outcomes of human interactions are always difficult to measure, and counselling presents additional challenges to researchers seeking to assess effectiveness. There are also some characteristics of counselling in criminal justice settings that complicate matters even further.

Egan (1994: 10) briefly reviews the research on 'the efficacy of helping', and notes two methodological problems. First, counselling is not something that is delivered, like a letter: the client has a significant influence on its outcome. The degree of clients' commitment to change is a complicating factor, and it is difficult to measure or to control for this experimentally. Secondly, counsellors are individuals too. Their methods and general effectiveness vary:

> Not all helpers are competent, and not all are committed. And even the competent have their lapses. . . . Variations in success rates typically have more to do with the therapist than with the type of treatment.
>
> (Egan 1994: 11)

These general difficulties apply to all research on effective practice in caring professions. In some areas, expensive, large-scale research has been undertaken (such as that into the treatment of sexual offenders). Some psychotherapy research has involved special training in particular treatment methods for the therapists whose work was being researched, and their results were then compared with those of a control group (Moras 1993). Counselling agencies do not generally command the resources needed for this kind of experimental research design, and it may be that a more qualitative style of investigation is in any case more appropriate to such settings. Certainly, most of the available research into the outcomes of counselling involves no assessment of the competence of those delivering it (McLeod 1995).

McLeod (1995) points to a number of other issues about research methodology in counselling. It is difficult to control for the training and the competence of the counsellors, and it is also hard to select comparable samples of clients in many counselling settings. Most counsellors do not specialize in a particular area of practice; they deal with the clients who come through the door. This makes it almost impossible to design studies that compare the outcomes of counsellors' work with one group of clients with the outcomes for similar 'untreated' individuals, which is one reason for the lack of evaluative material specifically looking at the effectiveness of counselling offenders.

Counsellors are rarely the only people working with a client, and many of the others (such as social workers, doctors, psychiatrists) will also be drawing upon counselling skills. In such cases, it is not possible to distinguish between the effects of the help given by different agencies and workers to the same client. If intervention has been helpful, which worker's involvement was decisive?

McLeod also points out that most of the research to date has either been small scale, or else it has been designed by other professionals whose assumptions and priorities might not be shared by the counsellors whose work is being evaluated (for example medical personnel, managers and psychologists). This certainly applies to most of the studies referred to in the present volume. Even where these difficulties can be overcome, many counselling agencies are monitoring their performance at the behest of funding bodies and government departments. Findings tend to be presented in a form easily assimilated by such sponsors, and the research design is fitted into this framework. This is not necessarily the optimum method of measuring effectiveness, which may be defined differently by funding bodies and the agencies themselves (see J. McLeod 1994).

To a large extent, then, 'The counselling outcome research literature is a story of what we don't know' (McLeod 1995: 198). It has been argued that genuinely rigorous research into the effectiveness of prison and probation work is equally scarce (Antonowicz and Ross 1994), although there is more of a tradition of such studies in those settings.

Counselling is a young profession, and is still in the process of developing research methods consistent with its values and methods. Psychotherapy, social work and other helping professions have been through the same process fairly recently. To the extent that part of their practice involves counselling, the research literature accumulated by these professions throws some light upon the question of the effectiveness of counselling. There is also a small but growing body of specifically counselling-based research, which is perhaps indicative of greater professional maturity on the part of counselling, demonstrating a commitment to self-evaluation.

Criminal justice settings introduce an added dimension when considering what works in counselling. Not only do clients see people other than counsellors, but their choice as to whether to take part in counselling is frequently taken out of their hands. The obvious example is the client who is before a court. Counselling in the community may have been recommended, but sentencers have other issues to consider in addition to the individual defendant's welfare. If they decide to imprison the client, this will have a considerable impact upon the availability of appropriate forms of counselling. On the other hand, if they sentence someone to receive community-based punishments, including a condition to undertake counselling, this raises a number of issues. The ethical questions for the counsellor have been considered in previous chapters. From a research point of view, a client sentenced to counselling presents different problems: how can outcomes be assessed, in comparison with other types of intervention, when the client enters the counselling relationship in such an unpromising way, coerced into receiving help?

The question of who judges the success of criminal justice interventions also complicates matters. The conventional measure of success is the rate at which members of a population of offenders receiving a particular form of treatment are subsequently convicted of further offences. This is an extremely crude measure, and it is impossible in practice to determine whether there are causal links between a particular type of intervention and the reconviction rate of those involved. At Grendon Underwood Prison, for example, the reconviction rates of successful members of therapeutic groups (those who stay the course) are a little lower than those of broadly comparable inmates of conventional prisons. American cognitive group counselling programmes also seem to reduce recidivism rates, according to one recent study (Watson and Stermac 1994). Much more striking than these statistics are the dramatic changes observed in the attitudes and behaviour of individual offenders after months of membership of the groups and of ready access to one-to-one counselling (Genders and Player 1995). Similarly, group work with sex offenders carried out by the probation service seems to be effective when properly targeted, but it has not until recently been systematically evaluated (Beckett *et al.* 1994, 1995).

It is obviously very important to know whether clients participating in some form of group or individual work are less likely to reoffend as a result, and the establishment of a research culture that encourages practitioners to ask such questions is long overdue. This does not mean, however, that every client's reconviction should be taken as a failure by the worker. Taking such events unduly personally is a common problem of newly qualified probation officers, for example. As they gain experience, they realize that their influence over clients is only one of a constellation of factors determining the likelihood of further offending. No matter how good one's relationship with clients, they may not think of coming for help when they are in a situation that tempts them to fall back into past patterns of behaviour. Rather than becoming depressed about their failure, staff need to be on hand to empower clients to face the consequences of their reoffending. Behaviour such as predatory sexual offending has deep roots. Although there is evidence, reviewed elsewhere in this chapter, that there are therapeutic approaches that can succeed in helping clients to change such behaviour, success is unlikely to come overnight in most cases. Counsellors working with offenders need to be persistent – and consistently available to help people pick up the pieces.

Effectiveness research itself has had rather an unwholesome influence in criminal justice settings, although those who carried it out cannot be blamed for this. In the prison and probation services, research findings have been oversimplified and misrepresented. This led to a widespread belief in the 1970s and 1980s that the research had found that 'nothing works', which did little to improve morale. Happily, this misconception has been corrected by more recent research (including a little-noticed study by one of the people who had previously published the famous 'nothing works' paper: see Martinson (1979)).

This episode is recounted in greater detail in Raynor *et al.* (1994) and in Raynor's earlier book (1985). Essentially, those committed to the rehabilitation of offenders made an enormous political mistake. They seized upon the idea that 'nothing works' as part of their arguments for due process approaches to sentencing and against imposing unfocused, possibly ineffective 'treatment' upon reluctant offenders, particularly those in prison. They were properly concerned about the civil liberties of clients and the need to ensure that any interventions in their lives were effective. The evidence of sociological research at around the same time was that clients were being unnecessarily labelled and the 'carceral net' was catching too many people too soon (Smith 1995). Unfortunately, the 'new right' was able to co-opt these arguments and use them against rehabilitation in general. Rehabilitative approaches were rapidly replaced with punitive methods, and the unfocused interventions with 'just deserts' sentencing (Arnold and Jordan 1995).

More recently, there has been a reconsideration of the effectiveness of various types of treatment available as part of the criminal justice system. Reviews of research in specific areas of practice have shown that counselling and other forms of intervention can be effective (see for example Marshall and Pithers' (1994) summary of the literature on sexual offenders, Sheldon's (1994) review of the literature relating to probation and youth justice, and the longer literature reviews by McIvor (1990), Cullen and Gendreau (1992) and by Raynor *et al.* (1994)). It is now generally agreed that some things do work, and that what is important for researchers is 'determining under what conditions rehabilitation works' (Antonowicz and Ross 1994: 97).

What has emerged from all these analyses is that effectiveness depends upon the use of the appropriate techniques with the appropriate clients, and that, in the criminal justice context, other variables such as the social and political situation also have to be taken into account. Effectiveness is inevitably judged by particular ethical standards (although these are not always made explicit). It might be argued that effectiveness is not a neutral concept, and that counselling must partly be measured with reference to whether it is equally effective with different social and racial groups (see the check lists of Raynor *et al.* (1994: 78–84), and also Dominelli *et al.* (1995), Howe (1993)).

If we want to show that counselling is an effective part of the rehabilitation of offenders, we must first be clear about what is meant by rehabilitating individuals (Raynor *et al.* 1994). Success rates will depend upon the definitions adopted: it is relatively easy to succeed in dealing effectively with offenders if they are merely required to make symbolic reparation for their offences (for example, by apologizing to victims after offender and victim have separately talked their feelings over with a probation officer trained in the use of counselling skills in such situations). If counselling interventions are more ambitious, success may be more elusive, but can still be achieved in a significant proportion of cases. Cognitive–behavioural group and individual work with some kinds of sexual offenders over a fairly lengthy period appear to be effective in reducing reoffending, to give an example from the limited research literature (Barker and Morgan 1993).

Some of the findings of the research in related fields may be transferable to counselling – but ideally, similar studies should be carried out in relation to specific counselling interventions in order to demonstrate their effectiveness convincingly. Individual counsellors can also use small-scale research methods to monitor their own practice, a procedure advocated for social workers (Everitt *et al.* 1992), teachers (Schon 1983) and counsellors (McLeod 1993) alike. At the very least, measures of client satisfaction should be routinely used, preferably long enough after the end of counselling for an objective view to be obtained (J. McLeod 1994: Chapter 8; McLeod 1995).

Generally speaking, counselling designed specifically for particular subgroups of clients seems to be 'more effective than generic counselling approaches applied with minimal accommodation to the primary care setting', according to McLeod (1995: 194) in a review of the evidence relating to counselling in general medical practice. This finding is similar to those of studies of work with offenders: carefully targeted, structured intervention based upon existing knowledge about what is likely to be effective does tend to work better than unfocused work (Raynor 1995).

Recently, several studies have reanalysed the effectiveness literature using meta-analysis to synthesize earlier findings (Haines 1990; McIvor 1990; Cullen and Gendreau 1992; Antonowicz and Ross 1994; Marshall and Pithers 1994; Underdown 1995). Considerable success has been claimed for programmes designed specifically for those offenders who are most likely to reoffend, and focused upon their offending and its contributory causes. Such intervention seems most likely to succeed where it is supported by agency management and delivered by appropriately trained staff who have access to sufficient resources.

Some such studies have gone further, arguing that programmes based upon cognitive and behavioural approaches are more effective than those based on other theories (Cullen and Gendreau 1992; Raynor 1995), and this is perhaps not surprising given the wide range of interventions potentially covered by the 'cognitive–behavioural' designation. Those who advocate working in these ways have suggested that 'programme integrity' is important: that is, that programmes are delivered in a consistent way that is monitored. Trained staff are required to deliver programmes in a consistent way. In its extreme form, this involves sessions being videotaped and tapes being returned to the organization that accredits the use of programme material, and that can withdraw authorization to deliver the programme if staff depart from the 'line' (see Neary 1992). Measures of this kind are employed because caring professionals find such rigidity uncongenial, but the advocates of cognitive–behavioural approaches believe strongly in the need to protect programme integrity. Most counsellors see themselves as 'eclectic or integrationist' rather than as delivering predefined material, but there is a trend towards 'manualized' staff training based upon handbooks containing detailed illustrative material (J. McLeod 1994: 138).

In practice, unless such drastic steps are taken, programmes are rarely delivered in a 'pure' form. For example, during a study tour of Canada in the spring of 1995, I was struck by the variety of imaginative approaches being used by probation staff in group work with sexual offenders. All ostensibly employed cognitive–behavioural techniques, and the designers of the programmes were at pains to emphasize the importance of programme integrity, but staff responded spontaneously to what was happening in the groups at any given time. In doing so, they called upon a repertoire of skills, including many not drawn from cognitive–behavioural theory. It is difficult to see how it could be otherwise without group work becoming mechanistic and boring for all the participants, staff and clients alike. Cognitive–behavioural techniques are powerful and effective, but need not be used inflexibly. What clearly is important is that staff expectations of such group work should be explicit, and that clients know what is intended and why (Raynor 1995). Some researchers do acknowledge that cognitive–behavioural approaches are likely to form part of a larger repertoire used by group workers (for example Cullen and Gendreau 1992; Antonowicz and Ross 1994).

WHAT WORKS IN COUNSELLING VICTIMS OF CRIME

The effectiveness of victim assistance has a research literature of its own. Unfortunately, the findings of these studies contradict one another in certain respects. One important finding is consistent: there is considerable evidence of victims' satisfaction with the services provided, although there is a lack of research about the most effective ways of helping people recover from victimization (Maguire 1991). Several summaries of the relevant research findings are available (Maguire 1991; Zedner 1994), so this section reviews this material only briefly.

Support for victims of crime in the UK has largely been provided by a single organization, Victim Support, and similar 'institutionalization and professionalization of victim services' have occurred in other countries. There is a danger that this can lead to the emergence and dominance of 'certain orthodoxies' about victim support

(Maguire 1991: 365). In particular, funding for alternative approaches may dry up, and the police may cooperate with the dominant group at the expense of others. Feminist approaches can suffer in this climate, as can other schemes critical of the orthodoxy. Victim Support has been alert to these dangers, and has established working relationships with Rape Crisis centres in most areas. It also assists emerging groups such as Support After Murder and Manslaughter (SAMM), which may at times take a different approach to that advocated by Victim Support.

Victims of crime are unlikely to express a need for counselling as such, but they do take it up gratefully when it is made available. Much Victim Support work is short-term (mostly consisting of a single meeting and concentrating upon practical help), but a minority of victims require support over a longer period.

There are few studies of the benefits of counselling. Surveys of victims indicate that a substantial minority would welcome counselling support, and that those who have received it feel they have benefited (Maguire 1991). Recently, schemes have begun to concentrate more effort on those who have suffered the effects of serious crime such as racial harassment, rape and murder, and counselling approaches designed to help victims of such offences have taken a higher profile within schemes. This is an important development in the light of long waiting lists for professional treatment (Neustatter 1994).

Many victims of serious crime benefit from exploring and understanding their grief and pain during counselling, but also want to take charge of the problem through self-help and campaigning activities. This need is often met by involvement in groups such as Victim Support, Rape Crisis and SAMM as volunteers, counsellors or committee members. Counsellors should recognize the benefits of such experience, and be flexible enough in their own practice to accommodate clients' differing forms of expression of their reactions to trauma (see Masters *et al.* 1988).

Generic counsellors are not always aware of the effects of secondary victimization: the criminal justice system makes life very difficult for the surviving relatives of murder victims and for people who have been raped, for example. This can go on for extremely long periods – for as long as the perpetrator lives in murder and some rape cases where someone has been sentenced to life imprisonment for the offence. At various stages, officials contact families under the provisions of the Victim's Charter, not always very sensitively (Kosh and Williams 1995). At some point, the offender is released from prison, sometimes to the area where the offence was committed, and the trauma is reawakened. Similarly, the treatment of raped women by the criminal justice system is often experienced as a form of victimization in itself. People who expect to receive sympathy and help find themselves subjected to further suffering. It is clearly important that counsellors are aware of these dimensions of victims' experience, and that they are in a position to help people decide how to proceed. While counsellors in the specialist agencies receive appropriate training, others will have no experience of these issues, and should consider referring clients to the specialists. They should avoid encouraging people to report offences if they are not aware of the stresses of court proceedings and available to support the client through these.

Victims of serious crime, and some victims of less serious offences such as burglary, are forced to reappraise their views of the world. It can suddenly seem a much more dangerous place, and a sense of loss of control leads some victims into depression. Counsellors working with victims of crime therefore need to be particularly alert to this, and to the danger in a minority of cases of suicide. Rapes in particular, but other serious crimes also, disrupt victims' relationships with families and partners. Again, counsellors can help by being aware of this possibility and facilitating discussion of such problems (Newburn 1993).

Much more research and development work is required before it will be possible to say with any confidence what kinds of intervention are most effective with victims of crime. For the time being, we do know that they perceive most counselling as beneficial, and that specialist victim counsellors are adapting their practice to reflect changing needs. There is also reassuring evidence in other fields that volunteer counsellors are as effective as professionals (J. McLeod 1994), and although no comparable studies have so far been undertaken with Victim Support, there is no reason to think that they would reach radically different findings.

SUMMARY

Counselling has been marginalized within the criminal justice context in recent years, for a variety of reasons. Attempts to cut costs and to pursue a harsher law and order agenda have tended towards a depersonalized service from probation officers, although they have vigorously opposed the trend and found creative ways to continue to employ their counselling skills for the benefit of offenders and victims of crime. Similar pressures have impinged unfavourably upon the police service, and progress towards improving the service given to victims of crime has been slow. The prisons have made some brave attempts to use counsellors and counselling skills constructively, but after a brief respite in the early 1990s following the publication of the Woolf Report (Woolf and Tumin 1991), pressure of numbers has restricted the scope for innovation or any kind of humane containment. Prison staff have been forced to concentrate upon warehousing inmates and maintaining security as best they can.

This does not sound like a very promising context for professional relationships between counsellors and others who work in criminal justice. All the same, counselling skills are valued in some parts of the system, and counsellors have an important role. Where they have become involved in the criminal justice system and adhered to their values, they have had a positive influence. This has resulted in improvements to prison regimes, in challenges being made to the dominant, macho subculture among prisoners and staff, in improved communications between agencies, and in more flexible ways of working. Counsellors and counselling agencies have had to be increasingly vigilant about maintaining appropriate boundaries between themselves and the criminal justice system, and there is no reason to think that the need for this will diminish in the near future. There is nevertheless considerable scope for positive relationships to continue to flourish, and criminal justice staff and their agencies have a great deal to learn from counselling.

All counsellors are likely to come into contact, directly or through clients, with the criminal justice system at one time or another. This book represents one resource which I hope will be of assistance, and this Chapter points interested counsellors towards a number of other possible sources of help.

In its final sections, it reviews some of the evidence about the effectiveness of counselling and of other services whose staff draw upon counselling skills. While there are considerable grounds for optimism, more research is needed before we can claim that counselling is indispensable in criminal justice settings. All counsellors working with criminal justice agencies and clients need to be cognisant of the political pressures to demonstrate effectiveness. In any case, it is surely part of basic professionalism to monitor one's practice: if the counsellor cannot demonstrate the effectiveness of counselling, who will?

In the final chapter, some of the issues raised during this discussion and throughout the book are explored further. The limitations of counselling within criminal justice are explored, and some changes which would improve existing arrangements are proposed.

· SIX ·

A critique of counselling in criminal justice

INTRODUCTION

As early as the mid-1960s, Halmos (1965: 7) was complaining that the lure of individual counselling was supplanting the attractions of resolving problems by taking political action: 'the counsellors have been responsible for a revival of interest in the rehabilitation of the individual, and a loss of interest in the rehabilitation of society'. This chapter reviews the present position concerning offender counselling, and poses questions about the appropriate relationship between counselling and an imperfect criminal justice system. While it would be unfair and irrational to expect counselling to solve all the problems and failures of the criminal justice system, does it have a role in addressing any of them? Is counselling in criminal justice settings just a good deed in a naughty world, the humane face of an unjust and oppressive system, or even itself a part of the problem? Or is it relevant to solving certain problems? Should we, in Halmos' phrase, maintain an interest in rehabilitating society?

In this chapter, I shall argue that counselling has a good deal to offer, but also that unless it changes in response to the demands and opportunities created by practice in criminal justice settings, it may come to be seen as irrelevant to the real problems facing criminal justice systems around the world.

There are some trends, discussed in earlier chapters, that affect counselling in criminal justice settings in ways that it is unlikely to be able greatly to influence. Counsellors need to be aware of these tendencies and ready to adapt their practice in ways that do least harm to their clients and least violence to professional ethics. One example is the politically motivated thrust of managerialism in public-sector agencies. In the criminal justice context, this has had largely negative effects (described in Chapter Five).

Managerialism has also had some positive benefits, for example the increased awareness among employers of the costs of losing trained staff and a corresponding increase in resources made available for workplace counselling. The connection between traumatization at work and subsequent absence through illness related to psychological distress has been recognized. The concern for efficiency has led directly to the provision of support and counselling to such staff, including police and fire personnel involved in disasters and prison officers affected by prisoners committing suicide (Liebling 1995). This has created a new role for counselling both within and beyond the criminal justice system, and such opportunities to relieve distress should be seized. They have a longer-term benefit than the immediate relief of distress if they also help staff avoid cynicism and the kind of protective distance from their clientele that can occur if they do not receive help in such circumstances. As Liebling (1995) points out, unsupported staff are more likely to leave their clients unsupported.

Similarly, harshly retributive 'new right' crime control policies are the product of potent social forces that counsellors are in no position to challenge directly. Yet some of the experiments and innovations described earlier in this book do call into question the assumptions underlying such policies. Some of the insights of feminist counselling have become accepted, even though they are profoundly subversive of the prevailing political orthodoxy. Others continue to excite debate and to question normative assumptions. The humanistic values of counselling (such as self-determination, respect for clients as dignified individuals with rights, non-judgementalism) stand in direct contradiction to retributive approaches to crime and deviance, but they need to be articulated and acted upon in practice if they are to be more than rhetoric (Beaumont 1995; Williams 1995a).

The incorporation of feminist ideas about masculinity into probation centre programmes is one example. Compulsory attendance at such centres was part of the drive to make community penalties more 'credible' and harsher, but probation staff have been able to introduce elements of individual counselling and group work that encourage male offenders to question their own underlying assumptions about aggression and about the role of women (examples of which are briefly described in Chapter Three). Counselling may be more difficult with a captive clientele, but this illustrates the scope for imaginative exploitation of the situation. Feminist ideas have also been successfully incorporated into much individual and group work with sexual offenders and men who are violent towards women (examples of this are given in Chapters Three and Four). Feminist counselling thus offers some possibility of altering the prevailing view of women's roles, although this is likely to be a very long-term project.

Counselling in criminal justice settings has not been so quick to integrate much of the new understanding offered by transcultural counselling, and this is an issue to which I return later in this chapter. Like social work in the UK in the 1950s, counselling draws much of its intellectual energy from North America. There is a danger that ideas that do not translate well from one cultural context to another may be adopted uncritically. As Woolfe *et al.* (1989: 10) have wryly pointed out, counselling is based upon theories developed on the west coast of America in the 1960s, and:

> For clients with plenty of money and in full employment, the process of moving towards self-actualization was and is a realistic goal. For clients who are unemployed, poor, and homeless, other objectives assume a higher status.

This is not to suggest that counselling cannot be adapted for use outside the United States or with poor, marginalized clients, but rather that such cultural differences cannot be ignored. It is dangerous to assume that approaches that are effective in one context can necessarily be applied in other countries without adjustment, as the discussion of cultural bias in Chapter Four illustrates.

THE DANGERS OF INDIVIDUALIZATION

Casework and counselling have long been attacked by radicals for individualizing social problems. The methods counsellors use need adaptation in criminal justice settings; clients are predominantly working class, many are black, and most are in financial need. Talk therapies based on the assumptions of middle-class white people need to be augmented with other strategies where criminal justice clients are concerned. The avoidance of political issues by counsellors and psychotherapists, combined with the belief in treating clients as unique individuals, can lead to a neglect of such additional techniques as group work, referral to self-help agencies, and advocacy on clients' behalf.

Criminal justice operates in most societies by individualization.

> This focus on the individual all but obscures the class issues involved in the law and its enforcement – for example the unequal distribution of wealth, the way the law bears heavily on working-class dishonesty and the effects of discriminatory policing. This concentration on differentness hides common causes and redirects possibilities for collective action into the search for individual solutions.
>
> (Walker and Beaumont 1981: 148)

It is therefore particularly important for criminal justice counsellors to avoid the negative aspects of individualization, while preserving and defending the positive ones. This is not easy when the discourse of individualism is so entrenched in counselling: as Meier and Davis put it (1993: 14), 'Individualize you must'. They are writing here about the need to adapt one's counselling style to the circumstances of each client, and to respect clients' individuality. There can be no quarrel with this, but if counsellors in criminal justice settings are truly to respect the individuality of their clients, they should be open to the possible benefits of combining individual work with other approaches. Otherwise, enormous and corrosive social problems are swept under the carpet. This applies not only to offender counselling, but also to work with victims of crime and with criminal justice personnel.

Where offenders are concerned, individualization runs the risk of ignoring structured inequality, police misconduct, class-biased legislation and so on. Victims need not only individualized counselling but opportunities to organize, to help themselves and one another, and to gain compensation and recognition of the harm done by offenders. The trend towards restorative approaches to victimization (discussed in Chapter Four) has developed in reaction to the failure of individualized methods. Stressed or traumatized staff have similar needs to those of victims of crime, as well as their undoubted requirement for individual counselling.

Insisting on the primacy of the one-to-one counselling relationship with these groups would disguise the social and political issues involved in criminal justice. In my view, counselling should be part of the attempt to construct a new paradigm for the resolution of the problems of the criminal justice system, not part of an attempt to cover them up! Open acknowledgement of the power differentials between counsellor and client is necessary in criminal justice settings (Hutchinson 1992; Williams 1995a). This issue does not arise in the same way in most other counselling contexts, but when working with offenders who are compelled to attend, it is thrown into sharp relief (see Chapter Four).

An overemphasis on the individual can lead to neglect of structural issues, and counselling has (until very recently) been peculiarly unaware of social divisions other than those based on gender. A comparison of counselling textbooks with those used in the training of probation officers or social workers is revealing: most counselling books assume a social consensus and many of them neglect to consider issues of race, class and disability. Social work and probation texts invariably address at least race and gender issues. It has recently been argued that a strength of counselling is its increasing willingness to recognize the social and structural aspects of individual problems (Woolfe *et al.* 1989). The literature does show a trend in this direction, but this has happened only in the last decade, and it is unclear to what extent the issues raised in research and in textbooks are being taken up in practice.

The assumption that contemporary societies are characterized by social harmony is particularly damaging in the criminal justice context, where clients are so painfully aware of inequalities. When counselling and criminal justice overlap, as in many of the case illustrations in this book, it is impossible to maintain an illusion of social consensus. The practice of counselling in criminal justice settings constantly throws up examples of injustice and inequality. There are ominous warnings implicit in the American literature of what could happen elsewhere if the dominant criminal justice assumptions were allowed to override counsellors' ideology of promoting self-actualization. If counsellors fail to take proper account of inequality and injustice, they will become unable to form helpful relationships with angry and embittered clients, who will doubt their good faith. It is difficult enough to transcend the barriers of class, gender or racial difference without creating additional blocks to communication by denying clients' experiences and situations.

Ultimately, counsellors outside the United States may find themselves arguing that 'directive counselling modalities allow the criminal justice counselor to . . . give orders and tell offenders what they must do' (Masters 1994: 113). They may even have to read offenders their rights before beginning some interviews (or interrogations), as advocated by Walsh (1992). As noted when these examples were used in Chapter Four, the American criminal justice system has somehow induced counsellors to practise in this way there. It would be better if counsellors withdrew from working with criminal justice clients, rather than tarnish their professionalism and values in similar ways.

THE NEGLECT OF RACE ISSUES

With some exceptions, counselling has failed properly to address race issues. The American counselling literature, although it has covered counselling by and with many different ethnic groups since the mid-1970s, largely fails (or refuses) to treat issues of oppression on grounds of race, disability or sexual orientation as issues of power. Books for students and practitioners of counselling that give due attention to this dimension of transcultural work have recently begun to become available elsewhere. The UK social work and probation literature may still be struggling with the complexity of race issues, but there is a much greater willingness to see them in terms of structural inequalities. This understanding needs to permeate not only the textbooks, but the training and practice of counsellors. Failing to address this will inevitably be taken by black clients as rejection (McLeod 1993). Even if and when an understanding of racism is properly incorporated in counselling practice, race will remain a barrier between white workers and black clients, who are bound to bring the pain and hostility engendered by racism into the counselling relationship with them (Devore 1987; d'Ardenne and Mahtani 1989).

Until then, trainers and practitioners need at the very least to commit themselves to stamping out bad practice. To assume that services are equally available to all, or that 'we are all the same underneath', is insufficient. This colour-blind approach is not much better than the assimilationist social policies of the 1960s, which were based on a belief that incomers should conform to the dominant culture and forget their own. Counselling that does not challenge such assumptions serves black clients badly, and there is evidence that they are more likely than similar white clients to drop out of treatment (McLeod 1993). More seriously still, colour-blind approaches by counsellors 'may victimize their clients further through their lack of understanding' (Ridley 1995: 5). 'Color-blind counselors relate to minority clients as though race is unimportant' (Ridley 1995: 68), which not only denies the clients' own experiences but leads to mistaken assessments and bad decisions.

Because of the racism endemic in criminal justice systems around the world (Hudson 1993; Mandamin 1993; Consedine 1995; Dominelli *et al.* 1995), race is a matter of central concern to people working with offenders. It has not hitherto been seen as such in the world of counselling, and this will have to change if counselling is to become part of the solution rather than part of the problem.

RESOURCES FOR ETHICAL PRACTICE

Throughout this book, questions of resources have inevitably been raised. Counselling organizations constantly identify new needs, but this is easier to do than finding the resources to meet them. The distribution of funding is not necessarily prioritized according to the urgency of clients' needs: much of it emanates from statutory sources, which are democratically accountable, and funding is likely to follow votes either directly or indirectly. Where funding is sought from charities and trusts, there is massive competition, and although trustees of such bodies may be more open minded about who deserves support, they are under increasing pressure from rising demand. Commercial funding is usually linked to a demand for publicity, which may cause ethical problems, and most criminal justice counselling agencies are unlikely to satisfy potential sponsors' requirements because their clients and policies are too controversial (see Tyndall (1993) for a fuller discussion of commercial funding).

Clients of criminal justice agencies are not the most popular of causes. While substantial funding has become available for (certain types of) victims of crime, finance for helping offenders is more difficult to obtain. Even counselling services for police officers have to compete with other demands for funding, and operational policing is likely to be a higher priority at times of budgetary restraint than staff care.

The inevitable need to make decisions about prioritizing one group of clients rather than another means that counselling cannot be available to all. Unfortunately, it has also led to decisions being made in a discriminatory way. For example, the politically popular Victim Support receives substantial central government funding, while the more controversial Rape Crisis centres receive none. At local government level, Victim Support in some areas receives official funding that has increased while support for Women's Aid and Rape Crisis has been cut. This reflects a process of dividing victims of crime into those seen as deserving help and the undeserving. As Mawby and Walklate have pointed out (1994), this simply reproduces the discretionary responses to need that characterized Victorian charitable giving. Clients wanting to go to Rape Crisis for help may find that there is no centre within easy reach, whereas there are Victim Support schemes covering every town in the UK. Clients arriving at their nearest Rape Crisis centre are likely to find it housed in a small, scruffy office and their counsellor may well have to take a turn on the rota to keep the premises clean.

Where a telephone service has been provided to help people who cannot get to the office, it may be possible to operate it only for a few hours each week.

A similar example relates to counselling services provided in prisons in England and Wales. While people in the community who asked to have HIV tests were routinely provided with pre- and post-test counselling, this service was not made available to prisoners until some years later. Either it was assumed that prisoners were less anxious about such tests, or they were seen as less deserving than people outside.

Where new counselling services have been developed in response to perceived needs, provision has sometimes been patchy because of shortage of funds. Thus Childline is unable to provide enough telephone lines or operators to take all the calls made to it by abused children. Similarly, the extension of the remit of Victim Support to encompass counselling for women who have been raped has had to await additional funding and is not yet happening on a national basis.

A further example is racial harassment. Victim Support is gradually extending its services to meet victims' need for counselling, but this is a recent development. Earlier self-help solutions to the problem were frowned upon by the police, and there is a suspicion in some quarters that the issue has been passed to a 'respectable' criminal justice agency in an attempt to discourage the development of black self-organization. Indeed, Victim Support experienced some difficulties when its pilot project for racial harassment victims was set up in London, because it was perceived as too closely aligned with the police (Kimber and Cooper 1991).

Counsellors cannot simply stand back and observe the kinds of trends identified here. If client need is unmet through lack of resources, it may be difficult to address this. Where needs are redefined or left unmet for political reasons, it will also be hard to do anything about it, but it is unethical to collude with the decision makers by doing nothing. The professions involved in counselling should at least draw attention to the processes involved in making such discriminatory decisions, and they should also do what they can to make it possible for colleagues in the affected agencies to practise professionally.

Ethical practice can take place only in a climate where clients are not discriminated against on the grounds of the political unpopularity of their particular needs. It follows from this that counsellors have a responsibility to support the provision of services to all in need, irrespective of the relative popularity of different client groups.

TRAINING NEEDS

If counselling is to increase its role in criminal justice settings, some changes may need to be made in the ways in which counsellors are trained. Counsellors already in practice and those on qualifying courses have training needs in relation to working in criminal justice settings, as do those employing counselling skills as social workers and probation officers.

As described in Chapters One and Two, training for the professions has shifted its emphasis towards competence-based approaches as part of an attempt to improve countries' abilities to compete in international markets. Although this might seem irrelevant to the training of counsellors, it has had a substantial effect upon all the professions in criminal justice. Where the training of social workers and probation officers is concerned, an unintended consequence was that 'people skills' began to be displaced by job-related aspects of the initial training curriculum. The courses' validating body, the Central Council for Education and Training in Social Work (CCETSW), no longer requires attention to be paid to the detail of how workers' relationships with clients are formed and maintained. Courses have responded by turning their backs on what was once the core of their curriculum, individual work with clients, and the trend towards case management has accelerated this process. This presents a threat and also an opportunity to those involved in counselling training.

The nature of the threat was identified by Dryden (1991: 4) when he warned that counsellor training must not become unduly preoccupied with skills training at the expense of 'therapeutic understanding'. The development and growth of counselling as a distinct discipline has occurred partly because counselling courses successfully occupied intellectual ground vacated by social work training. As social work education became increasingly skills focused, there was scope for counselling to concentrate upon developing students' therapeutic understanding. The increasing emphasis upon competence and case management rather than individual work with clients was at the expense of the moral and 'feely' aspects of social work training and practice.

Counselling, like social and probation work, is a profoundly moral endeavour, and this must be reflected in training courses. If it is not, there will be nothing to prevent counselling in criminal justice settings being co-opted by the kind of authoritarian populism that requires American prison counsellors to interrogate clients about offences and parole officers in some states to carry guns. Many counselling courses devote considerable attention to the ethics of the interview (how to avoid damaging or abusing clients, how to show positive regard for them as individuals) but very little to larger ethical issues such as the relevance of race, gender and class to counsellors' relationships with their clients. In the criminal justice context, these issues are crucial, along with other matters specific to the work setting. Counsellors working with offenders need to prepare for this by thinking through their views about punishment and justice, and developing the professional confidence to challenge bad practice by others.

The enormous opportunity for counselling training is the chance to move further into the ground vacated by social work courses. Some counselling training programmes are already finding that counsellors working in criminal justice are forming an increasing percentage of their intakes. Part of the increase has arisen from a recognition by some staff with social work qualifications that intensive work with particular client groups requires training and supervision in greater depth than current arrangements or their initial qualifying training provide. Experienced staff have begun to join counselling courses for professional development purposes. Probation officers trained on the new Diploma in Social Work courses to 'challenge offending behaviour' and 'punish in the community' increasingly feel that there is something missing from their repertoire. They want to work on the use of relationships. Many more students welcome the opportunity to study counselling part time over a number of years, rather than qualifying in social work all at once on a full-time course (although part-time and modular social work courses are increasingly becoming available in response to such demands). For voluntary counsellors, often working in hard-pressed non-statutory agencies, the time that counselling tutors are prepared to spend with them discussing their cases is a valuable addition to work-based supervision. Volunteers in some agencies receive most of their supervision in this way.

Other opportunities exist for counsellor trainers in the criminal justice field. Many of the agencies employing counsellors have training needs that are not being fully met, and some have considerable resources available to meet such needs. The smaller organizations may find it difficult to meet the cost of training their counsellors to develop new projects, but in some cases they are part of national bodies with separate funds. For example, it was noted in Chapter Two that Victim Support is trying to extend its work to provide a counselling service for the families of people who have been murdered and provide long-term help to raped women – but has so far been able to introduce it only in some parts of the UK. Locally based trainers may well be able to assist in meeting such needs.

MANAGERIALISM AND COUNSELLING IN CRIMINAL JUSTICE SETTINGS

The moral dimension of counselling has considerable potential for influencing policy. As discussed earlier in this chapter, it has had a positive influence in a number of areas, for example in the increasing provision of staff care services, and in the use of the insights of feminist counselling with male offenders. It may be that its humanistic values can also help to resist the worst effects of managerialism as they affect criminal justice clients (discussed in Chapter Five).

The positive potential of individualization, as long as structural issues are not ignored in the way described earlier in this chapter, is considerable. Managerialism deliberately attacks the concept and practice of professionalism, arguing that management is about control and professional autonomy threatens that control (Simiç 1995). Counsellors are better able than many of those working in criminal justice to defend their autonomy in making decisions about how they practice; they have a well established system of professional supervision and a wide range of theoretical approaches that are not accessible to lay control. At present, they are also independent of government, as most counsellors are not on the public payroll. They nevertheless have a fairly sophisticated system of accountability, although this is still voluntary and the title of counsellor is as yet unregulated – anyone can set themselves up as a counsellor.

The ease with which the professional status of the probation officer has been attacked in the UK (discussed in Chapter Two) shows how precious such autonomy is. Disciplines whose members work in large bureaucracies are very vulnerable to this kind of ideological assault, while the self-employed and self-regulated status of counsellors offers some protection. This autonomy is precious, and should be defended in the interests of clients. As Simiç (1995: 10) has pointed out, bureaucracies tend to try to gag their staff:

> Criticism is seen as criticism of the organisation and personal integrity a weaker link than loyalty and job security. There is, thus, a relationship between corporatism and lies (economies with the truth and other such euphemisms) that has no parallel in ethical professional practice, whatever the profession.

He gives the example of 'gagging' clauses in doctors' contracts with

National Health Service trusts, but the argument applies equally to professionals in the criminal justice system defending their respective codes of ethics and value bases against a management ideology that aims for hegemony.

Counsellors retain the freedom to work as they choose with clients, subject to certain ethical constraints, including in many cases a specific code of ethics. This means that practice can continue to develop unhindered by managerialization and its narrow definition of accountability (usually mainly financial in nature). If counselling can continue to become more professional in its approach without in the process also becoming bureaucratized, this will be in the interests of effective work with clients.

Even before the recent managerialist trend, bureaucratic structures effectively constrained creative and imaginative counselling practice (Brearley 1995). The notion of street-level bureaucracy might have been invented to describe the difficulties encountered by probation officers trying to engage in counselling with clients, for example those in prison. Clients interviewed about their probation officers' practice complain that the policies of probation services (including financial restrictions upon visiting) prevent a client-centred, personalized approach to through-care work. They express considerable dissatisfaction with bureaucratic and impersonal ways of working. One went so far as to compare probation officers with social security clerks (Williams 1992b, 1995b). Most counsellors are privileged in remaining outside a bureaucracy (although it may not always feel that way). They have considerable freedom of manoeuvre as a result.

LEGAL ISSUES IN COUNSELLING IN CRIMINAL JUSTICE SETTINGS

There are times when counsellors' lack of awareness of legal frameworks can be problematic – both within and outside the criminal justice system. There is a tendency to fail to recognize the legal aspects of clients' problems, or to assume that other professionals will already have engaged with them. Jenkins (1995a) found that a third of counselling courses teach no law, and suggests that counsellors tend to see policy and conflict in individual rather than structural terms. Some trainers feel that legal aspects of counselling are a matter for attention in the workplace rather than on courses, or that the law is learnt implicitly by discussion of ethics and values. When conflict is taking place within legal discourse, this approach can seem dangerously naive.

Jenkins (1994) gives a case study example of this, already mentioned in Chapter Five. A counsellor who had supported a client through first the disclosure and later the reporting to the police of a rape accompanied her client to court when the matter came to trial. The prosecution barrister was concerned that the counsellor's presence at court might undermine the client's credibility as a witness: the defence might seek to portray the client as unstable, or even to suggest that the counsellor had put words into her mouth. The counsellor had expected the trial to be a therapeutic experience for the client, achieving justice, whereas in fact the lawyers did all the talking and the client had no chance to say what she wanted to the judge. In the end, both client and counsellor were disappointed and upset by the experience of the court case.

The counsellor said later,

> There's a sense when you go to court, it will all just go through . . . It's a whole other world . . . I was just naive about all that . . . sometimes it might work . . . and other times it can be just as damaging . . . Now I know that it can be long, gruelling, complicated, and you won't necessarily get the result that you want, even though it's quite clear that you should.
>
> (Quoted by Jenkins 1994: 49–50)

She reflected that in future she would want to prepare a client very thoroughly for the decision about whether to take a case to court, making it clear that it was likely to be a difficult, lengthy and painful process. Her awareness of the complexity of legal issues and of the damaging effects of a gladiatorial system of deciding guilt or innocence will be helpful in her work with future clients, but this particular client would have been better served by a counsellor who did not learn the lesson at her expense. This is not a criticism of the counsellor herself, who clearly gave a caring and professional service. The training she had received simply did not equip her to work at the interface between counselling and criminal justice, or to recognize the legal aspects of a case. She was fortunate in having worked with a barrister who anticipated some of the problems, but more could have been done to prepare the client for the experience of the trial.

This is not an isolated case. In a straw poll of 25 counselling students in July 1995, only three of whom were working in criminal justice settings, I found that another seven had experience of counselling clients who had some kind of contact with the criminal justice system. These ranged from substance abusers who happened to be in prison to victims of car crashes who were pursuing compensation. Some of the counsellors drew successfully upon their previous experience (one had been a magistrate, another a prison officer, a third a psychiatric nurse and another had worked for the Crown Prosecution Service). Others sought advice from the police, the probation service or their supervisors. Several felt that their clients' dealings with the criminal justice system were being expertly dealt with by lawyers or other professionals, and feared to stray into areas where they themselves had little expertise. It may be that the use of case studies during training such as those shared by these students would increase counsellors' confidence in dealing with such cases. The present isolation of generic counselling from criminal justice is perhaps a somewhat unhealthy situation, particularly in view of Jenkins' comments about the relationship between law and the recognition of counselling as a legitimate occupation.

Counsellors need some degree of legal competence in order to practise professionally – and law is a component, however small, of most other professional training courses for caring work. It is an important characteristic of professionals that they recognize and act within the legal framework pertaining to their work. A more general awareness of criminal justice agencies, particularly of the courts, would seem to be a desirable addition to the training of counsellors. Many are now entering training in order to enhance the quality of their work with agencies such as Victim Support, Rape Crisis and with staff care services within the police and social services. Experiential training methods doubtless provide opportunities for such counsellors to share their practice knowledge with fellow students, and this is to be encouraged.

Only when counselling is recognized as having practice expertise in criminal justice contexts will counsellors' views about the need for changes in the law be likely to have any real impact. While the recognition of young people's and would-be parents' need for counselling in a few recent pieces of UK legislation is welcome, it does not approach the level of legal regulation and legitimation of other professions. Counsellors' initial training should clearly reflect – at the least – their legal powers as reflected in existing legislation. At present, 'Practitioners often talk about ethical issues without hard knowledge of the legal responsibilities on which they base their stance' (Jenkins 1995a: 13), and this is clearly potentially very dangerous. There is a series of references to counselling in recent legislation in England and Wales (Table 6.1).

Many counsellors will be surprised to find that their profession is recognized even to this extent by legislation in England and Wales. Such recognition provides a variety of opportunities, which should

Table 6.1 Statutory references to counselling in England and Wales (adapted from Jenkins 1993, 1994, 1995a; Robertson and Tudor 1993)

Year	*Statute*	*Provisions*
1976	Adoption Act	Provides for those who apply for access to their birth records to receive counselling
1989	Children Act	Updates the Adoption Act 1976 and also recognizes the role of counselling in work with children in need and their families
1990	Human Fertilisation and Embryology Act	Recognizes the role of counselling and of confidentiality within counselling
1990	NHS and Community Care Act	Does not explicitly refer to counselling, but counsellors have a role in meeting needs identified under its care management procedures, including care of former psychiatric patients
1991	Guidance and Regulations	Expand upon the Children Act, and specify circumstances in which counselling may be needed with reference to children's feelings of rejection by their parents, disability, sexual orientation, racial identity

be seized – assuming that counsellors are competent and qualified to practise in these settings (Robertson and Tudor 1993). In addition, competent practice must be based upon knowledge of the relevant law, and this has wider implications than those already raised with reference to working in criminal justice settings. All counsellors need to know about the legal constraints upon confidentiality if they are to form realistic contracts with their clients; they need to know and understand the implications of legislation against various forms of discrimination; they need to know about their own legal liabilities. Without this knowledge their practice, however caring and competent in other ways, may be seriously flawed.

CONCLUSION

It has already been observed in this chapter that counsellors do not tend to see problems in structural terms: they are more likely, by inclination and training, to seek solutions arising from their understanding of interactions between individuals. Some of the difficulties of working in the criminal justice system are simply not susceptible to solution on this level (although many practitioners achieve a great deal by networking: see Sampson and Smith (1992)). At times, counsellors may have to think in terms of community involvement, as in the case of the racial harassment project described in Chapter One, where the individual problems brought by clients were part of a web of connecting policy issues that had to be taken up with a wide variety of organizations. Another example, closer to the criminal justice system, is that of the sentencing patterns observed by Dominelli *et al.* (1995) and discussed in Chapter Two. A probation officer felt that a local court was sentencing in discriminatory ways, and professional ethics demanded that he take action. This particular case study also serves to illustrate the limitations of such activism in criminal justice settings: he was allowed to make his point, but then instructed to do so in future through the proper bureaucratic channels, which would probably tone down any subsequent attempt to hold the court accountable.

Earlier chapters have referred several times to the constant tension between care and control for counsellors and those using counselling skills in criminal justice. It is a difficult balancing act. Probation officers interviewed by Woodhouse and Pengelly (1991: 170):

> tended to feel accused by the law of being unwilling to control; by their colleagues in other helping professions, of being unwilling to care. Thus they were in the middle of a conflicting triangular dynamic.

So it is when counsellors in criminal justice settings try to take up issues on clients' behalf; they gain their credibility from their expertise in such matters, but they put it at risk if they begin to be perceived as campaigning for offenders' rights at the expense of those of victims, or vice versa. Such dilemmas are inherent in the counselling role in criminal justice settings, and there is no easy solution to them. It is nevertheless fascinating and rewarding to try to find answers that balance the needs of individual clients and those of society.

A recurring theme of this book has been the difficulty of practising counselling effectively in criminal justice settings. Resources are limited; counselling is marginalized by other priorities; issues of status and value conflicts get in the way of effective helping; clients may be hostile, resistant or challenging. These problems have been discussed in detail in previous chapters, and some of them are more easily surmountable than others. To what extent are counsellors responsible for overcoming such obstacles – and for trying to remove them?

The criminal justice system, by definition, operates within legal constraints. So, to a certain extent, do other settings in which counsellors work, and the law defines the extent to which counselling is recognized as a legitimate activity:

> The relationship of occupational groupings, whether professional or semi-professional, to the law, is a crucial index of their claim to recognition by society, and of their progress in achieving their desired status.
>
> (Jenkins 1994: 2)

Counselling, as a semi-profession (an occupation without all the trappings of a fully recognized profession such as medicine), seeks fuller legal recognition and regulation as part of its pursuit of social respectability and legitimacy. It is, in many ways, too ill-defined to be easily susceptible to state regulation and accreditation (Jenkins 1994) and there are compelling reasons for avoiding too much outside regulation. Counselling needs to retain its essential qualities and avoid the dangers of incorporation into bureaucratic frameworks. If it is to do so, a greater sophistication in relation to the legal context will, in my view, be a prerequisite.

Counselling is increasingly finding its way into legislation, and being specifically mentioned there as part of the solution to legal and emotional problems. Counsellors and those who train them have been rather slow to pick up on this recognition. The example of counselling in criminal justice contexts shows that much can be achieved where legal knowledge and counselling are successfully brought together. In future, such links will need to be made much more generally if progress towards recognition of the competence of counsellors to solve problems that have legal aspects is to continue.

Counsellors have a great deal to offer in criminal justice settings. If counselling is to achieve its full potential, counsellors in training and in practice will have to grapple with the kind of ethical dilemmas and practical problems discussed throughout this book. If they can be enabled to bring to such practice a greater awareness of the legal and structural aspects of individual cases, their contribution will be greately enhanced. This represents both an opportunity and a challenge for counsellors and for those who educate them. Failure to take the opportunity will lead to further marginalization, and undue incorporation into legal frameworks would threaten the independence and creativity of counselling. If an appropriate balance can be found, the potential rewards in terms of professional recognition and of opportunities to intervene effectively are enormous.

References

Allen, H. (1987) *Justice Unbalanced: Gender, Psychiatry and Judicial Decisions*. Milton Keynes: Open University Press.

Antonowicz, D. H. and Ross, R. R. (1994) Essential components of successful rehabilitation programs for offenders. *International Journal of Offender Therapy and Comparative Criminology*, 38 (2): 97–104.

Arnold, J. and Jordan, B. (1995) Beyond befriending or past caring? Probation values, training and social justice, in B. Williams (ed.) *Probation Values*. Birmingham: Venture.

Aston, J. W. (1987) Counseling men in prison, in M. Scher, M. Stevens, G. Good and G. A. Eichenfield (eds) *Handbook of Counselling and Psychotherapy with Men*. London: Sage.

Atherton, R. (1987) *Summons to Serve*. London: Geoffrey Chapman.

Aubrey, C. and Hossack, A. (1994) Contacting victims of life sentence crime. *Probation Journal*, 41 (4): 212–14.

Bailey, R. (1995) Helping offenders as an element in justice, in D. Ward and M. Lacey (eds) *Probation: Working for Justice*. London: Whiting and Birch.

Baker, P., Hussain, Z. and Saunders, J. (1991) *Interpreters in Public Services*. Birmingham: Venture.

Ballard, R. (1989) Social work with black people: what's the difference?, in C. Rojek, G. Peacock and S. Collins (eds) *The Haunt of Misery: Critical Essays in Social Work and Helping*. London: Routledge.

Barker, M. and Morgan, R. (1993) *Sex Offenders: A Framework for the Evaluation of Community-Based Treatment*. London: Home Office.

Barnes, G. G. and Henessy, S. (1995) Reclaiming a female mind from the experience of child sexual abuse, in C. Burck and B. Speed (eds) *Gender, Power and Relationships*. London: Routledge.

Barnett, M. A., Quackenbush, S. W., Sinisi, C. S., Wegman, C. M. and Otney, K. L. (1992) Factors affecting reactions to a rape victim. *Journal of Psychology*, 126 (6): 609–20.

Barnett, R. (1994) *The Limits of Competence*. Society for Research into Higher Education/Open University Press: Buckingham.

Beaumont, B. (1995) Managerialism and the probation service, in B. Williams (ed.) *Probation Values.* Birmingham: Venture.

Beckett, R., Beech, A., Fisher, D. and Fordham, A. S. (1994) *Community-Based Treatment for Sex Offenders: An Evaluation of Seven Treatment Programmes.* London: Home Office.

Beckett, R., Beech, T., Fisher, D. and Fordham, A. S. (1995) The therapeutic impact of sex offender treatment programmes. *Probation Journal,* 42 (1): 2–7.

Bolton, S. R. and Bolton, F. G. (1990) Meeting the challenge: legal dilemmas and considerations in working with the perpetrator, in A. L. Horton, B. L. Johnson, L. M. Roundy and D. Williams (eds) *The Incest Perpetrator: A Family Member No-one Wants to Treat.* Newbury Park: Sage.

Bond, T. (1992) Ethical issues in counselling in education. *British Journal of Guidance and Counselling,* 20 (1): 51–63.

Bracken, D. (1995) Cultural relevance and probation effectiveness in a Canadian Indian probation service. Paper given at the British Criminology Conference, Loughborough, July.

Braithwaite, J. and Daly, K. (1994) Masculinities, violence and communitarian control, in T. Newburn and E. A. Stanko (eds) *Just Boys Doing Business? Men, Masculinities and Crime.* London: Routledge.

Brearley, J. (1995) *Counselling and Social Work.* Buckingham: Open University Press.

Bridgewater, D. (1992) A gay male survivor of antigay violence, in S. H. Dworkin and F. J. Gutierrez (eds) *Counseling Gay Men and Lesbians: Journey to the End of the Rainbow.* Alexandria: American Counseling Association.

Bright, S. (1995) *HIV and AIDS in Prisons: Probation Responses.* Norwich: University of East Anglia Social Work Monographs.

Brown, A. (1984) *Consultation: An Aid to Successful Social Work.* London: Heinemann Educational.

Brown, A. (1994) Sex offender programme: a suitable case for treatment. *Prison Report,* 26: 4–5.

Brown, L., Christie, R. and Morris, D. (1990) *Families of Murder Victims Project: Final Report.* London: Victim Support.

Brown, S. L. (1991) *Counseling Victims of Violence.* Alexandria: American Association for Counseling and Development.

Buckman, R. (1992) *How to Break Bad News: A Guide for Health-Care Professionals.* London: Papermac.

Burnard, P. (1991) *Coping with Stress in the Health Professions.* London: Chapman and Hall.

Burnham, D., Boyle, J., Copsey, M., Cordery, J., Dominelli, L., Lamberts, J., Smallridge, M., Whitehead, V. and Willis, S. (1990) Offending and masculinity: working with males. *Probation Journal,* 37 (3): 106–11.

Burns, J. (1992) Mad or just plain bad? Gender and the work of forensic clinical psychologists, in J. M. Ussher and P. Nicolson (eds) *Gender Issues in Clinical Psychology.* London: Routledge.

Calhoun, K. S. and Atkeson, B. M. (1991) *Treatment of Rape Victims: Facilitating Psychosocial Adjustment.* New York: Pergamon.

Cameron, J. (1989) Bail schemes: the failure of reformism. *Probation Journal*, June: 78–81.

Carlen, P., Christina, D., Hicks, J., O'Dwyer, J. and Tchaikovsky, C. (1985) *Criminal Women*. Cambridge: Polity.

Cavadino, M. and Dignan, J. (1992) *The Penal System: An Introduction*. London: Sage.

Chaplin, J. (1988) *Feminist Counselling in Action*. London: Sage.

Clare, P. (1992) Post traumatic stress disorder: offender, victim and colleague as survivors. *Probation Journal*, 39 (4): 175–80.

Consedine, J. (1995) *Restorative Justice: Healing the Effects of Crime*. Lyttleton: Ploughshares.

Cooper, C. and Cartwright, S. (1994) Stress management interventions in the workplace: stress counselling and stress audits. *British Journal of Guidance and Counselling*, 22 (1): 65–74.

Corbett, C. and Hobdell, K. (1988) Volunteer-based services to rape victims: some recent developments, in M. Maguire and J. Pointing (eds) *Victims of Crime: A New Deal?* Milton Keynes: Open University Press.

Corden, J. and Clifton, M. (1983) The socially isolated prisoners project. *Research Bulletin* (Home Office Research and Planning Unit), 16: 45–8.

Cowburn, M. (1993) Groupwork programme for male sex offenders: establishing principles for practice, in A. Brown and B. Caddick (eds) *Groupwork with Offenders*. London: Whiting and Birch.

Cullen, F. T. and Gendreau, P. (1992) The effectiveness of correctional rehabilitation and treatment, in D. Lester, M. Braswell and P. Van Voorhis (eds) *Correctional Counseling*, 2nd edn. Cincinnati: Anderson.

Curran, L. (1987) AIDS in Prison, in B. McGurk, D. M. Thornton and M. Williams (eds) *Applying Psychology to Imprisonment*. London: HMSO.

Cyr, C. (1994) *Conceptual Model: Family Violence Programming within a Correctional Setting*. Ottawa: Family Violence Unit, Correctional Service of Canada.

d'Ardenne, P. and Mahtani, A. (1989) *Transcultural Counselling in Action*. London: Sage.

Davies, B. (1994) The Swansea Listener Scheme: Views from the Prison Landings. *Howard Journal*, 33 (2): 125–36.

Day, P. R. (1995) The turn of the tide: humanistic perspectives, social policy and social work. *Changes*, 13 (2): 77–81.

Denney, D. (1992) *Racism and Anti-racism in Probation*. London: Routledge.

Devore, W. (1987) Developing ethnic sensitivity for the counseling process: a social-work perspective, in P. Pedersen (ed.) *Handbook of Cross-cultural Counselling and Therapy*. New York: Praeger.

Dobash, R. P., Dobash, R. E., Cavanagh, K. and Lewis, R. (1995) Evaluating criminal justice programmes for violent men, in R. E. Dobash, R. P. Dobash and L. Noaks (eds) *Gender and Crime*. Cardiff: University of Wales Press.

Dominelli, L., Jeffers, L., Jones, G., Sibanda, S. and Williams, B. (1995) *Anti-racist Probation Practice*. Aldershot: Arena.

Dryden, W. (1991) *Dryden – on Counselling, Volume 3: Training and Supervision*. London: Whurr.

Duckworth, D. H. (1987) Professional helpers in disaster situations. *Bereavement Care*, 6: 26–9.

Duckworth, D. H. (1988) Disaster work and psychological trauma. *Disaster Management*, 1 (2): 25–9.

Earnshaw, J. (1993) Evolution and accountability: ten years of groups in a day centre for offenders, in A. Brown and B. Caddick (eds) *Groupwork with Offenders*. London: Whiting and Birch.

Edwards, J. (1995) Speech at the National Symposium on the Care and Custody of Aboriginal Offenders, Prince Albert, Saskatchewan, 15–17 February, mimeo.

Egan, G. (1994) *The Skilled Helper*, 5th edn. Pacific Grove, CA: Brooks/Cole.

Eisikovits, Z. C. and Edleson, J. L. (1989) Intervening with men who batter: a critical review of the literature. *Social Service Review*, 63 (3): 384–414.

Elias, R. (1993) *Victims Still: The Political Manipulation of Crime Victims*. London: Sage.

Emsley, C. (1994) Crime and crime control institutions, c.1770–c.1945, in M. Maguire, R. Morgan and R. Reiner (eds) *The Oxford Handbook of Criminology*. Oxford: Clarendon.

Everitt, A., Hardiker, P., Littlewood, J. and Mullender, A. (1992) *Applied Research for Better Practice*. Basingstoke: Macmillan.

Fagg, C. (1994) *To What Extent Does the Male Socialisation Process Provide an Explanation for Violence Within Intimate Relationships? Does Society (Specifically the Probation Service) Have a Responsibility to Confront This Issue?*, unpublished MA thesis, Department of Sociological Studies. University of Sheffield.

Family Service Unit (1985) *Access to Records*. London: Family Service Unit.

Faulkner, D. (1995) The Criminal Justice Act 1991: policy, legislation and practice, in D. Ward and M. Lacey (eds) *Probation: Working for Justice*. London: Whiting and Birch.

Fenby, J. (1992) Welfare reports: levels of agreement and parental views. *Probation Journal*, 39 (4): 185–91.

Fernando, S. (1986) Depression in ethnic minorities, in J. Cox (ed.) *Transcultural Psychiatry*. London: Croom Helm.

Fernando, S. (1988) *Race and Culture in Psychiatry*. London: Croom Helm.

Fielding, N. G. (1988) *Joining Forces: Police Training, Socialization, and Occupational Competence*. London: Routledge.

Fielding, N. (1994) Cop canteen culture, in T. Newburn and E. A. Stanko (eds) *Just Boys Doing Business? Men, Masculinities and Crime*. London: Routledge.

Flynn, N. (1995) Equality in the probation service, in D. Ward and M. Lacey (eds) *Probation: Working for Justice*. London: Whiting and Birch.

Foa, E. B., Rothbaum, B. O., Riggs, D. S. and Murdock, T. B. (1991) Treatment of post-traumatic stress disorder in rape victims: a comparison between cognitive–behavioral procedures and counselling. *Journal of Consulting and Clinical Psychology*, 59 (5): 715–23.

Ganley, A. L. (1991) Perpetrators of domestic violence: an overview of counselling the court-mandated client, in G. A. Harris (ed.) *Tough*

Customers: Counselling Unwilling Clients. Laurel: American Correctional Association.

Gardiner, D. (1989) *The Anatomy of Supervision*. Milton Keynes: Open University Press/SRHE.

Genders, E. and Player, E. (1995) *Grendon: A Study of a Therapeutic Prison*. Oxford: Clarendon.

Gibson, M. (1991) *Order from Chaos: Responding to Traumatic Events*. Birmingham: Venture.

Gilling, D. J. (1994) Multi-agency crime prevention: some barriers to collaboration. *Howard Journal*, 33 (3): 246–57.

Griffiths, C. T. and Patenaude, A. L. (1992) The use of community service orders and restitution in the north, in R. A. Silverman and M. O. Nielsen (eds) *Aboriginal Peoples and Canadian Criminal Justice*. Toronto: Harcourt Brace.

Haines, K. (1990) *Aftercare Services for Released Prisoners: A Review of the Literature*. London: Home Office Research and Planning Unit.

Halmos, P. (1965) *The Faith of the Counsellors*. London: Constable.

Halton, W. (1995) Institutional stress on providers in health and education. *Psychodynamic Counselling*, 1 (2): 187–98.

Handy, J. (1990) *Occupational Stress in a Caring Profession*. Aldershot: Avebury.

Hannah-Moffat, K. (1995) Feminine fortresses: woman-centered prisons? *Prison Journal*, 75 (2): 135–64.

Harper, L. and Charter, W. (1993) Proposal for the establishment of a native probation unit. Mimeo. Winnipeg: Department of Community and Youth Correctional Services.

Harris, G. A. (1991) *Tough Customers: Counseling Unwilling Clients*. Laurel, MD: American Correctional Association (pages not numbered).

Harris, G. A. and Watkins, D. (1987) *Counseling the Involuntary and Resistant Client*. Laurel, MD: American Correctional Association.

Hawkins, P. and Shohet, R. (1990) *Supervision in the Helping Professions*. Milton Keynes: Open University Press.

Hayman, V. (1993) Rewriting the job: a sceptical look at competences. *Probation Journal*, 40 (4): 180–3.

Hebenton, B. and Thomas, T. (1993) *Criminal Records*. Aldershot: Avebury.

Heidensohn, F. (1994) Gender and crime, in M. Maguire, R. Morgan and R. Reiner (eds) *The Oxford Handbook of Criminology*. Oxford: Clarendon.

Hicks, J. (1986) Probation and prisons – issues of orientation. Conference paper, in 'Probation: Engaging with Custody'. London: National Association of Probation Officers.

Hodgkinson, P. and Stewart, M. (1991) *Coping with Catastrophe*. London: Routledge.

Holdaway, S. (1983) *Inside the British Police*. Oxford: Blackwell.

Home Office (1990) *Victim's Charter*. London: HMSO.

Home Office (1995) *National Standards for the Supervision of Offenders in the Community*. London: Home Office Probation Service Division.

Horn, R. (1995) Not real criminals. *Criminal Justice Matters*, 19: 17–18.

House of Commons Home Affairs Committee (1989) *First Report: Racial Attacks and Harassment*. London: HMSO.

Howe, D. (1993) *On Being a Client: Understanding the Process of Counselling and Psychotherapy*. London: Sage.

Howe, D. (1994) Modernity, postmodernity and social Work. *British Journal of Social Work*, 24 (5): 513–32.

Hudson, B. A. (1993) *Penal Policy and Social Justice*. Basingstoke: Macmillan.

Humphrey, C., Pease, K. and Carter, P. (1993) *Changing Notions of Accountability in the Probation Service*. London: Institute of Chartered Accountants.

Hutchinson, E. D. (1992) Competing moral values and use of social work authority with involuntary clients, in P. N. Reid and P. R. Popple (eds) *The Moral Purposes of Social Work*. Chicago: Nelson-Hall.

James, A. L. and Hay, W. (1993) *Court Welfare in Action*. Hemel Hempstead: Harvester Wheatsheaf.

Jenkins, P. (1993) Counselling and the Children Act 1989. *Counselling*, 4 (4): 274–6.

Jenkins, P. (1994) *Counselling and the Law*. Unpublished MA dissertation, Department of Applied Social Studies. University of Keele.

Jenkins, P. (1995a) Training and the law within counselling and psychotherapy training within the U.K., in L. Mitchell (ed.) *The Law and the Training of Counsellors and Psychotherapists*. Report on Proceedings of Seminar organized by Wealden College, 5 April. Mimeo.

Jenkins, P. (1995b) Personal interview with the author.

Johnston, P. (1994) *The Victim's Charter (1990) and the Release of Life Sentence Prisoners: Implications for Probation Service Practice, Values and Management*. Cambridge: Institute of Criminology.

Johnston, P. (1995) The Victim's Charter and the release of long-term prisoners. *Probation Journal*, 42 (1): 8–12.

Jordan, B. (1995) Are new right policies sustainable? Back to basics and public choice. *Journal of Social Policy*, 24 (3): 363–84.

Jurgens, R. (1994) AIDS in prisons in Canada, in P. A. Thomas and M. Moerings (eds) *AIDS in Prison*. Aldershot: Dartmouth.

Kelly, R. J. (1990) Confidentiality issues with incest perpetrators: duty to report, duty to protect and duty to treat, in A. L. Horton, B. L. Johnson, L. M. Roundy and D. Williams (eds) *The Incest Perpetrator: A Family Member No-one Wants to Treat*. Newbury Park: Sage.

Kelly, T. A. (1990) The role of values in psychotherapy. *Clinical Psychology Review*, 10 (2): 171–86.

Kendall, K. (1993) *Literature Review of Therapeutic Services for Women in Prison*. Ottawa: Correctional Service Canada.

Kimber, J. and Cooper, L. (1991) *Victim Support Racial Harassment Project Final Report*. London: Community Research Advisory Centre, Polytechnic of North London.

Kinchin, D. (1993) Who cares for people who care? *Counselling*, 4 (2): 87.

Kosh, M. and Williams, B. (1995) *The Probation Service and Victims of Crime: A Pilot Study*. Keele: Keele University Press.

Kriner, L. and Waldron, B. (1988) Group counselling: a treatment modality for batterers. *Journal for Specialists in Group Work*, 13 (3): 110–16.

Lago, C. and Thompson, J. (1989) Counselling and race, in W. Dryden, D.

Charles-Edwards and R. Woolfe (eds) *Handbook of Counselling in Britain*. London: Tavistock/Routledge.

Lake, F. (1986) *Clinical Theology*. Abridged version of original 1966 edition. London: Darton, Longman and Todd.

Lee, A. and Searle, W. (1993) *Victims' Needs: An Issues Paper*. Wellington: Policy and Research Division, Department of Justice.

Liebling, A. (1995) Managing to prevent prison suicide: are staff at risk too?, in J. Kamerman (ed.) *Accountability in the Criminal Justice System: Views from Both Sides*. Illinois: Office of International Criminal Justice.

Life Support (1995) Newsletter of the Suicide Awareness Unit. London: HM Prison Service.

Lombardo, L. X. (1981) *Guards Imprisoned: Correctional Officers at Work*. New York: Elsevier.

Lombardo, L. X. (1985) Group dynamics and the prison guard subculture. *International Journal of Offender Therapy and Comparative Criminology*, 29 (1): 79–90.

Lorenz, W. (1994) *Social Work in a Changing Europe*. London: Routledge.

MacCarthy, B. (1988) Clinical work with ethnic minorities, in F. Watts (ed.) *New Developments in Clinical Psychology, Volume Two*. Chichester: Wiley/British Psychological Society.

McFarlane, A. C. (1994) Individual psychotherapy for post-traumatic stress disorder. *Psychiatric Clinics of North America*, 17 (2): 393–408.

McIvor, G. (1990) *Sanctions for Serious or Persistent Offenders: A Review of the Literature*. Stirling: Social Work Research Centre, Stirling University.

McKenzie, I. (1987) Policemen don't cry. *The Listener*, 12 March: 16.

McLaughlin, E. and Muncie, J. (1994) Managing the criminal justice system, in A. Clarke, A. Cochrane and E. McLaughlin (eds) *Managing Social Policy*. London: Sage.

McLeod, E. (1994) *Women's Experience of Feminist Therapy and Counselling*. Buckingham: Open University Press.

McLeod, J. (1993) *An Introduction to Counselling*. Buckingham: Open University Press.

McLeod, J. (1994) *Doing Counselling Research*. London: Sage.

McLeod, J. (1995) Evaluating the effectiveness of counselling: what we don't know. *Changes*, 13 (3): 192–200.

McLeod, J. and Cooper, D. (1992) *A Study of Stress and Support in the Staffordshire Fire and Rescue Service*. Keele: Centre for Counselling Studies, Keele University.

Machin, L. (1990) *Looking at Loss: Bereavement Counselling Pack*. Harlow: Longman.

Maguire, M. (1991) The needs and rights of victims of crime. *Crime and Justice, a Review of Research*, 14: 363–433.

Maguire, M. and Corbett, C. (1987) *The Effects of Crime and the Work of Victim Support Schemes*. Aldershot: Gower.

Mandamin, L. (1993) Aboriginal justice systems: relationships, in *Aboriginal Peoples and the Justice System: Report of the National Round Table on Aboriginal Justice Issues*. Ottawa: Ministry of Supply and Services Canada.

Mann, C. R. (1993) *Unequal Justice: A Question of Color*. Bloomington: Indiana University Press.

Marchant, C. (1993) Negative outlook – Counselling: women in prison. *Community Care*, 11 March: 24.

Marshall, W. L. and Pithers, W. D. (1994) A reconsideration of treatment outcome with sex offenders. *Criminal Justice and Behavior*, 21 (1): 10–27.

Martinson, R. (1979) New findings, new views: a note of caution regarding sentencing reform. *Hofstra Law Review*, 7: 243–58.

Mason, D. (1995) *Race and Ethnicity in Modern Britain*. Oxford: Oxford University Press.

Masters, R. E. (1994) *Counseling Criminal Justice Offenders*. Thousand Oaks: Sage.

Masters, R., Friedman, L. N. and Getzel, G. (1988) Helping families of homicide victims: a multidimensional approach. *Journal of Traumatic Stress*, 1 (1): 109–25.

Mawby, R. I. and Walklate, S. (1994) *Critical Victimology, International Perspectives*. London: Sage.

Maxwell, G. M. and Morris, A. (1993) *Family, Victims and Culture: Youth Justice in New Zealand*. Wellington: Institute of Criminology, Victoria University.

Meier, S. T. and Davis, S. R. (1993) *The Elements of Counselling*, 2nd edn. Pacific Grove: Brooks/Cole.

Menzies, I. E. P. (1960) A case-study in the functioning of social systems as a defence against anxiety. *Human Relations*, 13: 95–121.

Merchant, D. (1993) Gender: a management perspective, in P. Senior and B. Williams (eds) *Values, Gender and Offending*. Sheffield: PAVIC.

Miller, D. and Curran, L. (1994) HIV positive inmates: experiences and implications for prison HIV counsellors. *Prison Service Journal*, 94: 30–6.

Moerings, M. (1994) AIDS in prisons in the Netherlands, in P. A. Thomas and M. Moerings (eds) *AIDS in Prison*. Aldershot: Dartmouth.

Monger, M., Pendleton, J. and Roberts, J. (1981) *Throughcare with Prisoners' Families*. Nottingham: University of Nottingham Department of Social Administration and Social Work.

Moras, K. (1993) The use of treatment manuals to train psychotherapists: observations and recommendations. *Psychotherapy*, 30: 581–6.

Morris, A., Maxwell, G. M. and Robertson, J. P. (1993) Giving victims a voice: a New Zealand experience. *Howard Journal*, 32 (4): 304–21.

National Association for the Care and Resettlement of Offenders (1993) *NACRO Community Enterprises Housing Handbook*. London: NACRO Community Enterprises.

National Committee on Sex Offender Strategy (1995) *National Sex Offender Strategy*. Ottawa: Correctional Service Canada.

Native Clan Organization (1995) Aboriginal sex offenders symposium presentation. Mimeo. Winnipeg: NCO.

Neary, M. (1992) Some academic freedom. *Probation Journal*, 39 (4): 200–2.

Nellis, M. (1995) Probation values for the 1990s. *Howard Journal*, 34 (1): 19–44.

Neustatter, A. (1994) No help in time of trauma. *Independent on Sunday*, 4 December.

Newburn, T. (1993) *The Long-Term Needs of Victims: A Review of the Literature*. Home Office Research and Planning Unit Paper 80. London: HMSO.

Newburn, T. and Stanko, E. A. (1994) When men are victims: the failure of victimology, in T. Newburn and E. A. Stanko (eds) *Just Boys Doing Business? Men, Masculinities and Crime*. London: Routledge.

Newman, J. (1994) The limits of management: gender and the politics of change, in A. Clarke, A. Cochrane and E. McLaughlin (eds) *Managing Social Policy*. London: Sage.

Newman, J. and Clarke, J. (1994) Going about our business? The managerialization of public services, in A. Clarke, A. Cochrane and E. McLaughlin (eds) *Managing Social Policy*. London: Sage.

Northumbria Probation Service (1993) *The Northumbria Probation Service and Work with Victims*. Newcastle upon Tyne: Northumbria Probation Service.

O'Dwyer, J. and Carlen, P. (1985) Josie: surviving Holloway and other women's prisons, in P. Carlen, *et al.*, *Criminal Women*. Cambridge: Polity.

Padel, U. (1995) HIV, AIDS and probation practice, in B. Williams (ed.) *Probation Values*. Birmingham: Venture.

Padel, U. and Stevenson, P. (1988) *Insiders*. London: Virago.

Padel, U., Twidale, R. and Porter, J. (1992) *HIV Education in Prisons: A Resource Book*. London: Health Education Authority/SCODA.

Parris, K. C. (1968) Casework in a prison setting. *Probation*, 14 (2): 36–40.

Pearson, G., Sampson, A., Blagg, H., Stubbs, P. and Smith, D. (1989) Policing racism, in R. Morgan and D. J. Smith (eds) *Coming to Terms with Policing*. London: Routledge.

Pence, E. and Paymar, M. (1993) *Education Groups for Men who Batter: the Duluth Model*. New York: Springer.

Perry, J. (1993) *Counselling for Women*. Buckingham: Open University Press.

Priestley, P. (1981) *Community of Scapegoats: the Segregation of Sex Offenders and Informants in Prison*. Oxford: Pergamon.

Proctor, B. (1991) On being a trainer, in W. Dryden and B. Thorne (eds) *Training and Supervision for Counselling in Action*. London: Sage.

Ratigan, B. (1989) Counselling in groups, in W. Dryden, D. Charles-Edwards and R. Woolfe (eds) *Handbook of Counselling in Britain*. London: Tavistock/Routledge.

Raynor, P. (1985) *Social Work, Justice and Control*. Oxford: Blackwell. (Revised edn, 1992. London: Whiting and Birch.)

Raynor, P. (1995) Evaluating probation: the rehabilitation of effectiveness, in T. May and A. Vass (eds) *Working with Offenders: Issues, Contexts and Outcomes*. London: Sage.

Raynor, P., Smith, D. and Vanstone, M. (1994) *Effective Probation Practice*. Basingstoke: Macmillan.

Reeves, H. and Wright, M. (1995) Victims: towards a reorientation of justice, in D. Ward and M. Lacey (eds) *Probation: Working for Justice*. London: Whiting and Birch.

Reeves, J. B. (1995) Exploring differential occupational stress and the male sex role. *Free Inquiry in Creative Sociology*, 13 (1): 5–9.

Resick, P. A. and Schnicke, M. K. (1993) *Cognitive Processing Therapy for Rape Victims: A Treatment Manual*. Newbury Park: Sage.

Richards, D. (1994) Traumatic stress at work: a public health model. *British Journal of Guidance and Counselling*, 22 (1): 51–64.

Ridley, C. R. (1995) *Overcoming Unintentional Racism in Counselling and Therapy: A Practitioner's Guide to Intentional Intervention*. London: Sage.

Robertson, G. and Tudor, K. (1993) Counselling in the context of community care. *Counselling*, 4 (3): 188–90.

Root, A. and Davies, S. (1995) *On the Line: A Review of the Training Needs of Rape Crisis Centres*. London: Allen Lane Foundation.

Ross, R. and Fabiano, E. (1985) *Time to Think: a Cognitive Model of Delinquency Prevention and Offender Rehabilitation*. Johnson City, TN: Institute of Social Sciences and Arts.

Rutherford, A. (1993) *Criminal Justice and the Pursuit of Decency*. Oxford: Oxford University Press.

Salter, D. (1990) Lockerbie and after: an examination of the myths and metaphors of managers and workers in a disaster. *Changes*, 8 (4): 311–21.

Salter, D. (1995) Personal interview with the author, 21 July.

Sampson, A. (1994) *Acts of Abuse: Sex Offenders and the Criminal Justice System*. London: Routledge.

Sampson, A. and Smith, D. (1992) Probation and community crime prevention. *Howard Journal*, 31 (2): 105–19.

Sampson, A., Stubbs, P., Pearson, G. and Blagg, H. (1988) Crime, localities and the multi-agency approach. *British Journal of Criminology*, 28 (4): 4478–93.

Sampson, A., Smith, D., Pearson, G., Blagg, H. and Stubbs, P. (1991) Gender issues in inter-agency relations: police, probation and social services, in P. Abbott and C. Wallace (eds) *Gender, Power and Sexuality*. Basingstoke: Macmillan.

Scherdin, L. (1994) AIDS in prisons in Norway, in P. A. Thomas and M. Moerings (eds) *AIDS in Prison*. Aldershot: Dartmouth.

Schon, D. A. (1983) *The Reflective Practitioner: How Professionals Think in Action*. London: Temple Smith.

Scott, M. J. and Stradling, S. G. (1992) *Counselling for Post-Traumatic Stress Disorder*. London: Sage.

Senior, P. (1993a) Racial attacks and the probation service, in D. Woodhill and P. Senior (eds) *Justice for Young Black People*. Sheffield: PAVIC.

Senior, P. (1993b) Groupwork in the probation service: care or control in the 1990s, in A. Brown and B. Caddick (eds) *Groupwork with Offenders*. London: Whiting and Birch.

Shaw, R. D. (1995) *Chaplains to the Imprisoned: Sharing Life with the Incarcerated*. Binghamton, New York: Haworth Press.

Sheath, M. (1990) 'Confrontative' work with sex offenders: legitimised nonce bashing? *Probation Journal*, 37 (4): 159–62.

Sheldon, B. (1994) Social work effectiveness research: implications for probation and juvenile justice services. *Howard Journal*, 33 (3): 218–35.

Sheldon, B. (1995) *Cognitive–Behavioural Therapy: Research, Practice and Philosophy*. London: Routledge.

Sim, J. (1994) Tougher than the rest? Men in prison, in T. Newburn and E. A. Stanko (eds) *Just Boys Doing Business? Men, Masculinities and Crime*. London: Routledge.

Simiç, P. (1995) What's in a word? From social 'worker' to care 'manager'. *Practice*, 7 (3): 5–18.

Smith, D. (1995) *Criminology for Social Work*. Basingstoke: Macmillan.

Smith, J. (1989) *Misogynies*. London: Faber.

Snarey, J. R. (1985) Cross-cultural universality of social–moral development: a critical review of Kohlbergian research. *Psychological Bulletin*, 97 (2): 202–32.

Sparks, R. (1994) Can prisons be legitimate? *British Journal of Criminology*, 34: 14–28.

'T', A. (1988) Feminist responses to sexual abuse: the work of the Birmingham Rape Crisis centre, in M. Maguire and J. Pointing (eds) *Victims of Crime: A New Deal?* Milton Keynes: Open University Press.

Tarleton, P. (1995) (Lindholme Prison Chaplaincy) Personal interview with the author, 19 May.

Taylor, M. (1995) Feminist psychotherapy, in M. Walker (ed.) *Peta: A Feminist's Problem with Men*. Buckingham: Open University Press.

Tehrani, N. and Westlake, R. (1994) Debriefing individuals affected by violence. *Counselling Psychology Quarterly*, 7 (3): 251–9.

Thomas, P. A. (1994) AIDS in prisons in England and Wales, in P. A. Thomas and M. Moerings (eds) *AIDS in Prison*. Aldershot: Dartmouth.

Thomas, T. (1988) Confidentiality: the loss of a concept? *Practice*, 2 (4): 358–72.

Thomas, T. (1995) *Privacy and Social Services*. Aldershot: Arena.

Toch, H. and Klofas, J. (1982) Alienation and desire for job enrichment among correction officers. *Federal Probation*, 46 (1): 35–44.

Tyndall, N. (1993) *Counselling in the Voluntary Sector*. Buckingham: Open University Press.

Tyndall, N. (1994) Personal correspondence with the author, 14 December.

Underdown, A. (1995) *Effectiveness of Community Supervision*. Manchester: Greater Manchester Probation Service.

Ussher, J. (1990) Professionals don't cry. Death and dying in AIDS psychology. *Changes*, 8 (4): 284–93.

Vachon, M. L. S. (1987) *Occupational Stress in the Care of the Critically Ill, the Dying and the Bereaved*. New York: Hemisphere.

Varah, C. (1980) *The Samaritans in the 80s*. London: Constable.

Varley, M., Williams, B. and Williams, J. (1995) Through the looking glass: marking reassessed. *Social Work Education*, 14 (1): 7–23.

Victim Support Bedfordshire (undated; 1990?) *Final Report*. Bedford: Children as Victims of Crime Project, Victim Support Bedfordshire.

Victim Support (1995) *The Rights of Victims of Crime*. London: Victim Support.

Walker, H. and Beaumont, B. (1981) *Probation Work: Critical Theory and Socialist Practice*. Oxford: Blackwell.

Walker, M. (1990) *Women in Therapy and Counselling*. Milton Keynes: Open University Press.

Walsh, A. (1992) *Correctional Assessment, Casework and Counseling*. Laurel, MD: American Correctional Association.

Ward, D. (1995) Finding the balance, in D. Ward and M. Lacey (eds) *Probation: Working for Justice*. London: Whiting and Birch.

Ward, D. and Lacey, M. (eds) (1995) *Probation: Working for Justice*. London: Whiting and Birch.

Watson, R. J. and Stermac, L. E. (1994) Cognitive group counselling for sexual offenders. *International Journal of Offender Therapy and Comparative Criminology*, 38 (3): 259–70.

Wilkie, M., Ferrante, A. and Susilo, N. (1992) *The Experiences and Needs of Victims of Crime in Western Australia*. Nedlands: University of Western Australia Crime Research Centre.

Williams, B. (1991) *Work with Prisoners*. Birmingham: Venture.

Williams, B. (1992a) *Bail Information: An Evaluation of the Scheme at HM Prison Moorland*. Bradford: Horton.

Williams, B. (1992b) Caring professionals or street-level bureaucrats? The case of probation officers' work with prisoners. *Howard Journal*, 31 (4): 263–75.

Williams, B. (1994) The history of probation work with prisoners. *Social Services Research*, 2: 53–4.

Williams, B. (ed.) (1995a) *Probation Values*. Birmingham: Venture.

Williams, B. (1995b) Towards justice in probation work with prisoners, in D. Ward and M. Lacey (eds) *Probation: Working for Justice*. London: Whiting and Birch.

Williams, B. (1996) Social Work with Prisoners, in G. McIvor (ed.) *Working with Offenders*. London: Jessica Kingsley.

Williams, B. and Eadie, T. (1994) The contribution of prison-based bail information schemes to better jobs. *Prison Service Journal*, 93: 27–30.

Woodhouse, D. and Pengelly, P. (1991) *Anxiety and the Dynamics of Collaboration*. Aberdeen: Aberdeen University Press.

Woolf, Lord Justice and Tumin, Judge Stephen (1991) *Prison Disturbances April 1990*, Cmd 1456. London: HMSO.

Woolfe, R., Dryden, W. and Charles-Edwards, D. (1989) The nature and range of counselling practice, in W. Dryden, D. Charles-Edwards and R. Woolfe (eds) *Handbook of Counselling in Britain*. London: Tavistock/Routledge.

Worrall, A. (1995) Equal Opportunity or Equal Disillusion? The Probation Service and Anti-Discriminatory Practice, in B. Williams (ed.) *Probation Values*. Birmingham: Venture.

Yarmey, A. D. (1988) Victims and witnesses to deadly force. *Canadian Police College Journal*, 12 (2): 99–109.

Young, A. and McHale, J. V. (1992) The dilemmas of the HIV positive prisoner. *Howard Journal*, 31 (2): 89–104.

Zedner, L. (1994) Victims, in M. Maguire, R. Morgan and R. Reiner (eds) *The Oxford Handbook of Criminology*. Oxford: Clarendon.

Zimmer, L. (1987) How women reshape the prison guard role. *Gender and Society*, 1 (4): 415–31.

Index

COUNSELLING AND SOCIAL WORK

Judith Brearley

Social work is perennially in the public eye, and interest in counselling has never been greater. But these activities are changing rapidly in response to new needs and resource limitations, and their complexity is not easy to grasp even by those involved. This book looks at how the specific context of social work shapes the nature of counselling in terms of both opportunities and constraints. How can social workers integrate the counselling dimension of the job with other roles expected of them? What training, supervision and support do they need? How do they collaborate with other professions? Above all, how do they effectively deal with people's private troubles, subjective feelings and disrupted relationships (the traditional concern of counselling), whilst simultaneously fulfilling statutory requirements and involving themselves in the contentious politics of social provision? A disturbing situation is revealed, in which such role conflicts, coupled with media pressure and policy changes, are undermining the professional competence and confidence of social workers, thus depriving the most needy people of help. A fresh understanding of insights from counselling is seen as providing a partial answer to this serious state of affairs.

Contents

160pp 0 335 19002 2 (paperback)

COUNSELLING FOR YOUNG PEOPLE

Judith Mabey and Bernice Sorensen

This book gives a wide picture of the diversity of counselling services available to young people in Britain today, with special focus on schools and young people's counselling services. It sets these services in their historical context and describes how they have evolved. The book puts forward theoretical models for working with young clients and discusses counselling issues as they relate to work with this age group. In addition it considers some of the pitfalls counsellors may encounter in working alongside other professionals and within agencies. It includes discussion on ethical issues, non-discriminatory practice, confidentiality and child protection. The book is enlivened by case material and by examples of good practice and interesting initiatives from around the country. It will be of particular interest to counsellors, teachers, youth workers, social workers and counselling students interested in working with this age group.

Features

- Illustrated throughout with case material
- Wide discussion of ethical issues
- Examples of good practice and new initiatives
- Gives theoretical models for counselling young people

Contents

160pp 0 335 19298 X (paperback)

COUNSELLING FOR WOMEN

Janet Perry

Although few in number, organizations which provide counselling services for women have had a tremendous impact on our current understanding of women's psychology and the issues women explore in counselling. Through her examination of these organizations, Janet Perry highlights the unique emphasis they place on the importance of how services are provided and their exploration of the dynamics of the working relationships of women counsellors. The organizations included in the book range from Women's Aid to Women's Therapy Centres and their services are considered in the context of counselling women. The study shows that through a self-reflexive examination of their organizational processes, these agencies have come to a greater understanding of the ways in which women working with women create non-hierarchical and cooperative endeavours, much needed in our individualistic and competitive society. The book illustrates the conflicts that arise when both modes seek to exist within one organization – Family Service Units – and the struggle all the agencies have to legitimize these ways of working to a male dominated system from which funding is often sought. Recommended reading for all those involved in counselling and psychotherapy, this book illustrates some of the practical outcomes of these alternative working models.

Contents

128pp 0 335 19034 0 (paperback)